The Fall of
Roman Britain

The Fall of Roman Britain

and Why We Speak English

John Lambshead

PEN & SWORD HISTORY

First published in Great Britain in 2022 by
Pen & Sword History
An imprint of
Pen & Sword Books Ltd
Yorkshire – Philadelphia

ISBN 978 1 39907 556 5

A CIP catalogue record for this book is
available from the British Library.

Typeset by Mac Style
Printed and bound in the UK by CPI Group (UK) Ltd,
Croydon, CR0 4YY.

Pen & Sword Books Limited incorporates the imprints of Atlas,
Archaeology, Aviation, Discovery, Family History, Fiction, History,
Maritime, Military, Military Classics, Politics, Select, Transport,
True Crime, Air World, Frontline Publishing, Leo Cooper, Remember
When, Seaforth Publishing, The Praetorian Press, Wharncliffe
Local History, Wharncliffe Transport, Wharncliffe True Crime
and White Owl.

For a complete list of Pen & Sword titles please contact

PEN & SWORD BOOKS LIMITED
47 Church Street, Barnsley, South Yorkshire, S70 2AS, England
E-mail: enquiries@pen-and-sword.co.uk
Website: www.pen-and-sword.co.uk

Or

PEN AND SWORD BOOKS
1950 Lawrence Rd, Havertown, PA 19083, USA
E-mail: Uspen-and-sword@casematepublishers.com
Website: www.penandswordbooks.com

Contents

Introduction

In science, complicated questions commonly lead to simple answers. Conversely, simple questions often can only be answered in a complex way if, indeed, they can be answered at all. Consideration of deceptively simple questions, such as 'the origin of species?', 'how did life start?', 'why does time only run one way?', or 'what is gravity?' produce cascades of new more specific queries, the investigation of which changes our view of reality.

The development of the English language, now the global *lingua franca*, is rather well known. But a simpler question remains: why do we, the lowland inhabitants of the island of Britain, the Roman Britannia, speak English at all?

The end of empire in the island of Great Britain was both more abrupt and more complete than in any of the other Roman provinces. When the fog clears and Britain re-enters the historical record, we find the island dominated by a new culture that speaks a language that is neither Roman nor indigenous British Brythonic and with a pagan religion that owes nothing to Romanitas or native British practices. Indeed, it is uncontroversial to note that, at least initially, Anglo-Saxon England derived little either culturally or materially from the Roman world.

Other ex-Roman provinces of the Western Empire in Europe showed two consistent features conspicuously absent from the lowlands of Britain: the dominant language was derived from the local Vulgar Latin and the dominant religion was a Christianity that looked towards Rome. This leads naturally to the question 'what was different about Britannia?' What was it about the province that led to a different outcome from the rest of continental Roman Western Europe as exemplified by modern France, Spain, Portugal, Italy and Romania?

A further anomaly in our understanding lies in the dating mismatch between historical and archaeological data of the Germanic migrations and the latest genetic evidence. The answer to England's unique early history may lie in resolving this paradox.

The boundaries of the Roman Empire in the east stabilised along a defendable zone between the Roman and Persian/Parthian empires – in short, a balance of military power along a geographic feature between two organised states. In the south, the Empire stopped at the edge of the coastal zone and Nile river where there was a sharp transition between arable land and largely uninhabitable desert.

In the north, the limits of Empire were fixed in position by forces more akin to those found in northern China (Heather 2005). The frontiers of an empire facing a power vacuum tend to align with an intermediate zone of part arable and part pastoral land, a region which is not of itself capable of supporting imperial armies but is conveniently located close enough to an arable zone such that food can be transported and stored at the frontier both to support long term garrisons and supply field armies mounting time-limited campaigns across the frontier.

As Heather (2005) pointed out, a socioeconomic line not some ethnic/linguistic division such as conquered Gauls and free Germans fixed the Roman Empire's northern frontier. La Tène culture on western arable land generated enough agricultural surplus to support an organised, sophisticated society with specialised social classes, such as warrior-aristocrats and priests-cultural leaders, while the Jastorf culture to the east had no such food surplus.

A similar situation applied in Britain. The south and eastern arable lowlands with which the pre-invasion Romans were most familiar supported a sophisticated culture not unlike that of the La Tène, but the upland zones to the west and north were a different matter.

In continental Europe a Germanic/Romantic linguistic divide still largely follows the Imperial boundary. In Britain a similar post-Roman linguistic boundary emerged with native Brythonic spoken in the west and places outside the Empire, but novel Germanic dialects dominated the arable lands despite Vulgar Latin surviving immediately across the Channel.

The pattern is not that of a degradation of Romanitas as it jumps the Channel to expire at a British frontier zone, but a sharp discontinuity, an intrusive bulge of Germanism into a Romanitas that still echoes along the British upland frontiers with the persistence of Latin as an elite, 'official', written (and possibly spoken) language and the survival of Christianity. The two are of course interlinked as the Church used Latin.

The superficial data suggests that the difference between post-Imperial outcomes of Britain and the Continent was not simply quantitative such as degradation of Romanitas caused by the Channel but some qualitative difference. Either Britannia was always in some way different from its neighbouring provinces and/or something unique and probably uniquely horrible happened in the British lowlands in the early fifth century.

Once we would have had no doubts as to the nature of this awful event. Brought up on a diet of Bede, Gildas and King Arthur stories, we 'knew' that powerful warrior kings stormed ashore at the head of large, heavily armed warbands, sacking the cities, putting the villas to the flame and their Romanised inhabitants to the sword. Modern archaeological research tells a different tale. Pryor (2004) reflects a consensus of many modern historians when he writes, 'To me the notion of Anglo-Saxon invasions is an archeologically absurd idea.'

To quote Fleming (2010), 'By 420 Britain's villas had been abandoned. Its towns were mostly empty, its organised industries dead, its connections with the wider Roman world severed; and all with hardly an Angle or Saxon in sight.'

And it happened in a single generation.

Many other academics have in one form or another addressed this issue of what might have precipitated such a catastrophe – and it was a catastrophe not an adjustment or an evolution (Ward Perkins, 2005). I would like to revisit the ruin of Roman Britain from the perspective of a natural scientist, a biologist who has worked in the fields of evolution, biodiversity and ecology. This discipline is not such a stretch from that of the study of human history as one might imagine, because people are biological organisms. They and their cultures exist and develop in a biosphere which is subject to change, sometimes rapid or even catastrophic change, that has and will impact human civilisations.

Natural science investigative processes are themselves historical, using techniques not dissimilar from those employed by historians and archaeologists to determine the past. Until we have the benefit of time machines, current patterns, 'fossilised' evidence recovered from the present world, and what we think we can deduce about processes gleaned from similar but never identical events, are the only data available to investigate the past.

We now have enormous amounts of genetic data from high-throughput molecular analysis allowing statistical analysis in a way that is rarely possible with historical data. However, the molecular data suggests that German immigrants and the indigenous British did not start admixing until around AD 800 or later, three hundred and fifty years after the first Germanic settlers arrived in Britain.

Here I summarise the data gathered by historians, archaeologists, climatologists and biologists and see if some synthesis can be created to help us understand (i) why Britannia was so comprehensively ruined, (ii) why the molecular data fails to correlate with archaeological data when dating the Saxon migrations, and (iii) why the inhabitants ended up speaking English.

Chapter 1

Set in a Silver Sea

The Biogeography of Britain

A key difference that strikes one immediately when comparing Britain with other European Roman provinces is that Britain is an island, by far the largest European island covering an area of around 230,000km², but an island nonetheless. The nearest European islands in size are also in the North Atlantic, for example Iceland at just over 100,000km² and Ireland at about 84,000km². In contrast, the largest islands with which the classical world was familiar are Sicily and Sardinia in the Mediterranean at approximately 26,000 km² and 23,000km².

In this chapter I will discuss the ramifications of being a large Atlantic island, notably the degree of isolation from the continent. Seas are both a barrier and a highway – a barrier because they act as a block on coordinated movement, and a highway because waterways were the only way to routinely move bulk products before the invention of the steam engine. Broadly speaking, the more technically sophisticated a people, the more a seaway becomes a highway rather than a barrier.

Somewhere around 450,000 years before the present, a catastrophic geological event caused a profound and long-term effect on European and global human history. A vast continental ice sheet extended from southern Scandinavia to northern England, blocking the exit of major rivers flowing out of north-western Europe into the Atlantic. Melting ice created a giant glacial lake in what is now the southern North Sea (Gupta *et al*, 2007).

The lowest point of land containing this vast water body stood 30 metres above the current sea level, the Weald–Artois chalk-ridge. The rivers kept flowing and at some point, probably during a storm precipitating heavy rainfall and blowing a gale that formed waves on the surface of the lake, water started to trickle over this chalk ridge down into the river valleys that drained south-west. The trickle rapidly grew to a torrent cutting through the chalk – and the torrent became a megaflood. The power of that biblical event carved a deep, straight, valley leaving a permanent geological imprint. These days we call it the Straits of Dover.

The ice withdrew and the great rivers drained north again until about 180,000 years ago. Once again, ice dammed the rivers creating a new glacial lake with its southern bank to the north of the straits of Dover, a bank possibly consisting of moraine dropped by previous glaciation. Inevitably the water also overflowed this barrier, creating another megaflood that deepened and widened the Straits.

In periods of glaciation when sea levels were low as happened just twelve thousand years ago, a great river flowed south-west down to the Bay of Biscay through a wide valley between what is now the English West Country and the Brest Peninsula. The Rhine, Meuse, Scheldt and Thames, Rother, Somme, Solent and Seine added to this river until it carried half the drainage of Western Europe. But in warmer periods when sea levels were higher, the continent was doomed to be cut off from the island of Britain by the English Channel (Gibbard, 2007). The most recent land bridge from the continent to Britain submerged about eight thousand years ago.

We still live with the environmental, social and political consequences of that geological separation event.

The English Channel and North Sea act as a biogeographic barrier to the movement of species, gene flow and culture. For example, there are more than fifty species of snake considered to be native to Europe but just two to Britain – the common European adder (*Vipera berus*) and the barred grass snake (*Natrix natrix*) – while Ireland has no native snake species at all: St Patrick banishing Ireland's snakes after a forty-day fast is a charming but regrettably untrue story.

With respect to human society, isolation by waterway impedes the flow of both genes and culture. Barbujani and Sokal (1990), using a new methodology rather wonderfully named 'wombling', identified 33 genetic boundaries in Europe of which 31 are consistent with linguistic boundaries. Mountain ranges coincide with 4 of these boundaries but no fewer than 18 align with waterways.

Our species apparently did not reach the large island of Madagascar until two thousand years ago – and the evidence is that they came the 400 kilometres from Indonesia rather than the relatively short crossing from Africa because of the direction of winds and currents. At sea the shortest way is not always the easiest. Of course, the 33 kilometres across the Straits of Dover is somewhat more manageable even if the 350km from the Netherlands to East Anglia is on a similar scale.

Once our species invented boats, waterways became permeable barriers, but the ability to cross a waterway is not enough to mount a seaborn invasion where a host of load-carrying vessels are required to navigate a seaway with enough confidence to maintain a convoy and place an army or sizable warband on a specified section of coast within a specified time. This raises an immediate question. Could an Anglo-Saxon chieftain/king build and navigate an ocean-capable fleet sufficient to transport a warband large enough to overcome organised local resistance?

Crossing the Channel

About twenty pre-Roman period Bronze Age boats have been discovered in Britain and some are considered to be open-sea capable. The 'Ferriby' boats, discovered at the Humber estuary and dating from 4,000 years before present were possibly capable of crossings to the continent while the Dover Bronze Age boat dated at around 3,500 years before present is generally considered seagoing. The Dover boat was between ten and twelve metres long and two metres wide – room for paddlers sitting two abreast. The construction resembles the Ferriby boats, oak planks lashed together using yew.

Could the Dover Boat have crossed the Channel? On a good day with an experienced crew and a navigator with a firm grasp of the treacherous Channel tidal currents it probably could. The journey would be a risky business, but then matelot has always been a precarious profession.

Germanic migrants or warbands had access to naval technology somewhere between the Dover boat and the later superbly designed ocean-going Viking vessels that represented a revolution in naval technology. The famous early fourth-century Nydam boat from southern Denmark was clinker built from oak, about twenty-three metres long and two metres wide, giving room for a crew of thirty oarsmen. Unlike a Viking longboat it had no mast or sails, lacking the longboat's keel.

The AD 430 coastal 'boat-burial' at Fallward of what appears to be a wealthy, Germanic, retired Roman soldier with maritime associations (first a soldier then a sea raider?) gives an idea of the type of boat available to the inhabitants of north-west Germany in the migration period: a photograph was published in the March-April 2020 edition of *British Archaeology*.

The seventh-century (?) Gredstedbro ship, what there is of it, also lacks a longboat keel so had no mast. Similarly, some twenty pairs of oarsmen crewed the twenty-seven-metre Sutton Hoo ship, dated to the early seventh century. It also lacked a mast or full longboat-type keel. The Oseberg ship burial, dated to AD 834, although the boat may be two or three decades older, contains the first recognisable longboat.

The evidence suggests that non-Roman North European peoples both before and immediately after the Roman period had access to large seagoing rowing boats but not ocean-capable sailing boats. These rowing boats could cross the North Sea and English Channel in favourable conditions but were extremely labour intensive with a high crew to load capacity. They made acceptable small raiding boats because the crew and cargo (warriors) were the same thing but were limited to transporting small high value goods when employed as traders.

Similarly, they had limitations as migration vessels, probably being restricted to one family group per boat when their essential property, children, farmstock etc is included.

Vessels like the Nydam and Gredstedbro boats would be slow and vulnerable to the current and wind conditions found in the North Sea and English Channel. Predictable navigation, arriving at set places at set times, was not possible. Accordingly, the boats would have found it extremely difficult to maintain anything like a military invasion convoy. Single raiding vessels could reach more or less the right area in more or less an acceptable time, then row along the coast to deposit a party of twenty or so warriors onto a suitable target to carry out a 'smash and grab' raid.

The number of raiders in one boat were sufficient to overwhelm the defensive forces immediately available to, say, a Roman villa but then they would flee back out to sea with the loot before reinforcements in the form of a detachment of the Roman army could come to the villa's aid. However, this is quite different from organising an invasion fleet, supplying it while waiting for favourable conditions, and keeping it together in transit so as to arrive in something resembling a solid mass at more or less the same place at more or less the same time.

Wealthy Germanic veterans from the Roman army like the Fallward warrior undoubtedly observed and quite possibly travelled in Roman ocean-capable sailing ships of the Rhine and Channel fleets, so this raises the question why they did not commission similar vessels when they returned home? The answer is probably that being a passenger in a boat gives little insight into how to construct the vessel, especially to warriors whose skills lay in fighting rather than marine engineering.

Any complex technology requires a suitable infrastructure of manufacturing locations and technology, resource pipelines, and – not least – a viable body of people with the requisite skills. Sailing warships in the Mediterranean had a pedigree that went back to the Bronze Age and were part of an engineering skill set that included the know-how to construct complex buildings and water-control technology such as aqueducts, drainage and canals. While it can be astonishing to the modern observer what ancient peoples could achieve with ridiculously simple tools, no evidence for the necessary technological capacity exists east of the Rhine.

Siege machines require a technology of similar complexity to sea-going sailing ships that 'barbarian' armies of this period noticeably failed to master. For example, the Germanic army that fought the Gothic War of AD 376–382, fought and decisively defeated a Praesental army (an Imperial field army usually led by a ruling Caesar or Augustus) at Adrianople killing the Emperor Valens in the process, from which we can deduce that barbarian pitched battlecraft could be competitive with that of Rome. Nevertheless, the inhabitants of Adrianople repulsed repeated assaults by the same Goths on their city.

One of the Gothic leaders, Fritigern, declared he 'kept peace with walls' and plundered the countryside instead despite the greater concentration of portable loot within city walls. Had the Goths the skill set to construct and employ siege machines then I doubt they would have 'kept peace with walls'.

While on this topic, emperors attempted to prevent barbarians from acquiring ship-building skills. For example, Bishop Asclepiades in AD 419 petitioned the Emperor to release men who had been arrested for betraying shipbuilding secrets to barbarians. The barbarian maritime raids in the Aegean in the third century demonstrate the potential threat.

It is instructive to look at the history of attempted invasions of Britain, whereupon it becomes clear how difficult it could be. The first invasion fleet that we know of was that of Julius Caesar in 55 BC.

Caesar's legate, Decimus Junius Brutus Albinus, fought the naval Battle of Morbihan in Quiberon Bay against the Gallic Veneti fleet: the Veneti lived on fortified peninsulas along the south coast of what is now Brittany (ancient Armorica). They controlled the tin trade with southwest Britain using heavily built ships powered by oars and sail.

Caesar describes these vessels in his *Gallic Wars*:

> 'Their keels were considerably flatter than those of our own ships, that they might more easily weather shoals and ebb-tide. Their prows were very lofty, and their sterns were similarly adapted to meet the force of waves and storms. The ships were made entirely of oak, to endure any violence and buffeting. The cross-pieces were foot-thick beams, fastened with iron nails as thick as a thumb. The anchors were attached by iron chains instead of cables. Skins and pieces of leather finely finished were used instead of sails.'

As far as I know we do not have any remains of a Veneti ship, but the later Romano-Celtic 'Blackfriars' ship, dated to around AD 150, was probably not dissimilar. The vessel was 14 metres long and 6.5 metres wide. She probably sank after a collision while carrying Kent ragstone for the construction of Londinium's riverside wall (Marsden, 1994). Useful reconstructions can be found in Elliott (2016).

Caesar's 55 BC invasion fleet consisted of eighty ships, enough to transport two legions, plus eighteen more ships following on behind with the cavalry. It included both transports and warships, according to the following quote from the *Gallic Wars*:

> '[Caesar] commanded the ships of war (which were less familiar in appearance to the natives, and could move more freely at need) to remove a little from the transports, to row at speed, and to bring up on the exposed flank of the enemy; and thence to drive and clear them off with slings, arrows, and artillery. This movement proved of great service to our troops; for the natives, frightened by the shape of the ships, the motion of the oars, and the unfamiliar type of the artillery, came to a halt.'

The warships' description is that of typical classical war galleys, and it is implied that the transports were both different to the warships and familiar to the British so were probably Veneti ships.

The 55 BC invasion suffered from Channel conditions. Storms delayed and scattered the cavalry transports driving them back to Gaul. The beached galleys of the landed infantry filled with water due to the Romans underestimating the scale of Channel tides and transports riding at anchor were driven against each other by more storms.

The point is that despite the considerable organisation skills of the Roman army and their access to sophisticated sailing/oared vessels, the 55 BC invasion was anything but plain sailing and failed when the army's logistics broke down – they ran out of food when the fleet was damaged. The cavalry transports got no closer than within sight of the beachhead before being blown back to the Continent.

The 54 BC invasion was an altogether more substantial undertaking, with 800 ships carrying 5 legions and 2,000 cavalry in purpose-built, shallow-drought, modified Veneti invasion vessels. But once again storms damaged the anchored invasion fleet, logistical problems obliging Caesar to declare victory and retreat.

To underline the point, the last attempted invasion of Britain using sailing ships was by a French Republican fleet in 1797. Despite using vastly superior ships to anything available to classical civilisations, contrary winds forced the invasion fleet to land troops at Fishguard rather than Bristol and the whole enterprise descended into farce.

The first successful military invasion of Britain that we know of was that of Claudius in AD 43 – although his campaign may have been built upon an unsuccessful attempt by Caligula in AD 40 according to a bizarre story told by Seutonius.

'[Caligula] drew up his army on the shore of the ocean, with his ballista and other engines of war, and while no one could imagine what he intended to do, on a sudden commanded them to gather up the sea shells, and fill their helmets and the folds of their dress with them, calling them "the spoils of the ocean due to the Capitol and the Palatium." As a monument of his success, he raised a lofty tower, upon which, as at Pharos…'

Our knowledge of the life and times of Caligula is so heavily distorted by hostility from ancient writers that it is almost impossible to separate fact from an ancient version of a Whitehall farce, but the salient points are that the invasion was called off after Caligula had gone so far as to build a lighthouse and port facilities at Boulogne as well as the construction of transports (Elliott, 2016) so the intent was probably serious even if the execution failed.

The Claudian attempt was on a massive scale, transporting four legions plus auxiliaries, around 40,000 men, with their equipment and logistical needs. This would have included 3,000 tonnes of grain. Grainge (2005) suggests 900 boats would have been required – presumably mostly Romano-Celtic transports with an escort of war galleys much like Caesar's second invasion fleet. The crews had to be reinforced by sailors from as far away as the *Classis Misenensis* in Italy.

Post-Roman Frankish warlords in Gaul no doubt had access to the resources and technology to mount a military invasion of Britain – but we know they did not – and the people who later buried a king at Sutton Hoo could not.

Conclusions

To conclude: a key to understanding Britain's uniqueness in the Roman Empire was its geographical situation – an island of considerable size separated from the continent by dangerous seas that were only navigable for part of the year – and not entirely safe even then.

The sixth- and seventh-century Germanic peoples outside Romanitas lacked the technology, resources and organisational skills to mount anything resembling an organised invasion of Britain by a powerful warlord. They could build large rowing boats that could cross the sea at unpredictable rates to an unpredictable destination, transporting small raiding warbands, high value goods, and migrating families – permitting a constant flow of cultural artefacts, genes and people between Britain and the continent in both directions – just as they had from the Bronze Age onwards.

Chapter 2

Evidence from Bodies

Isotope Analysis

Essentially there are two chemical analytical techniques available for investigating the origins of the people of Britain. The first is 'stable isotope analysis' and the second is the relatively new science of 'molecular biology', especially nucleic acid analysis.

Isotope analysis relies on the subatomic properties of atoms. The number of protons, also called the atomic number, in an atom's nucleus defines an element. For example, carbon has an atomic number of 6, oxygen 8 and strontium 38. However, the nuclei of atoms of the same element can vary in their number of neutrons. These variants are called 'isotopes' of the element.

Isotope analysis can be extremely useful in archaeology. For example, carbon dating relies on a ratio of isotopes of carbon. Carbon 14, with six proton and eight neutrons, is formed in the upper atmosphere by cosmic rays hitting nitrogen atoms. Carbon 14 is radioactive, i.e. it breaks down. One of its neutrons decays to a proton creating an atom of nitrogen, atomic number 7.

The time taken for any particular atom to decay is not constant but is governed by probability so half the atoms in any large batch of Carbon 14 will have decayed after 5,700 years (+/- 40 years). It's a bit like the old schoolboy trick question of 'if a helicopter descends such that it drops half the distance to the ground every ten seconds, when will it land?' The answer is 'when it runs out of fuel'.

Living organisms take up Carbon 14 throughout their lives so have a fixed ratio of ^{14}C to stable carbon isotopes, mostly ^{12}C. But when that organism dies it stops absorbing new ^{14}C so this ratio changes predictably with time as the ^{14}C decays. The measured ratio, with a bit of fiddley calibration for local variation, can be used for dating organic material over a range of tens of thousands of years.

Stable isotope analysis relies on the ratio of isotopes that are unchanged over time. Different locations and ecosystems have different stable isotope ratios so this property can be used to determine the source of an artefact compared to where it was discovered.

There is a very early Anglian cemetery at West Heslerton, Yorkshire, dating back to the late fifth- or early-sixth centuries. Archaeologists distinguish two separate ethnic groups in the burials: around 80 per cent are 'British' and the remaining 20 per cent 'Anglian' with artefacts similar to those found in Denmark. Budd *et al* (2004) performed oxygen isotope analysis on twenty-four individuals buried in the cemetery. Of these only four had grown up as children on the continent, probably in Scandinavia.

What is interesting is that all four were women, one a juvenile. Gilke (pers. comm.) points out that women have tended to move more than men and have been more likely not to return because they 'marry out'. Marrying out is vital for humans to avoid accumulation of harmful genetic mutations, and in low population groups this means travel. The human genome is a mess, but that is a story for another day. Also of significance is that these continental women had a lack of grave goods compared to other females in the group, suggesting they may have been slaves or at least low status. These were not by any stretch of the imagination warriors from either a ruling Anglo-Saxon warband or a unit of *foederati* mercenaries.

Similarly, Hughes *et al* (2014) analysed tooth enamel (which forms in childhood) from nineteen individuals from the early Anglo-Saxon cemetery at Wally Corner, Berinsfield, in the Upper Thames Valley, Oxfordshire. This location is interesting because it is not on the coast but artefacts associated with Anglo-Saxons have been found that are dated to the mid or even to the first quarter of the fifth century i.e. very early. Traditionally, these artefacts were attributed to Saxon *foederati*, allies, by some Romano-British ruling authority (e.g. Dickinson, 1977) and, of course, the Kingdom of Wessex started in this location. Hughes *et al* (2014) found no isotopic evidence to support the existence of *foederati*. Of the nineteen remains analysed, oxygen isotope ratios pointed to only one individual of continental origin.

The data are limited but we have to go with what we have and isotopic analysis suggests that certainly some early cultural Anglo-Saxons were not invaders or *foederati* but grew up from children locally.

Ancient Genomes

Britain depopulated during the last ice age, humans only permanently returning across a land bridge from about 11,600 years ago in the Hoxnian when there was a sharp rise in temperature and the ice retreated. These hunter/gatherers probably followed herds of reindeer and horses into Britain.

Molecular mitochondrial analysis of the Cheddar Man – human remains found in Gough's Cave in the Cheddar Gorge and dated to about 9,500 years ago – show the U5 haplotype (a haplotype is a section of DNA on one chromosome so inherited from one parent). This marker is common among Mesolithic Europeans, especially those from north-east Europe, but it is also found in Iberia. The first permanent inhabitants of Britain were therefore part of a widespread, homogenous group of probably wide-ranging hunters (Sánchez-Quinto et al, 2012).

The first farming communities in Britain, heralding the Neolithic, started about 6,000 years ago, a whole thousand years after the Continent, so either the British developed their conservative social habits early or the English Channel acted as a barrier. Brace et al (2019) assembled genome-wide data from 6 Mesolithic and 67 Neolithic individuals found in Britain from around 10,500 to 4,500 years ago. Their analysis shows a strong affinity between British and west European Mesolithic hunter-gather populations but also reveals the arrival of newcomers in the Neolithic with a genetic link to Iberia, suggesting that the Neolithic revolution was introduced into Britain from the Eastern Aegean region via Iberia. These Neolithic Mediterranean-derived newcomers largely replaced the earlier Mesolithic hunter-gatherers from northern Europe.

At this point it is worth noting that the Darwinian phrase 'survival of the fittest' has a very specific meaning in biology. It simply means 'those with the greatest reproductive success', which may be down to all sorts of reasons not least sheer chance. Misinterpretation of the word 'fittest' to mean 'best' rather than 'successfully prolific' has led to people putting a pseudoscientific gloss on all sorts of batty social theories such as eugenics. In biological terms, the 'Mediterranean' immigrants were 'fitter' because their farming technology allowed them to be prolific breeders, or, to put it another way, they could support larger populations. Whether the newcomers were more or less 'fit' in any particular human subjective interpretation of the word is of no relevance.

Haak *et al* (2015) employed a high-throughput genomic analysis using DNA hybridisation for genomic-wide large-scale analysis. High throughput can produce data of similar value to archaeological and linguistic methods. For example, Haak *et al* (2015) present data on more than twice as many ancient Eurasian individuals than all previous data put together. They targeted 394,577 single nucleotide polymorphisms (SNPs) – known as a '390k capture'.

Single nucleotide polymorphisms (SNPs), pronounced 'snips', are single small lengths of DNA that vary between people so may be used as markers to recreate phylogenetic relationships, i.e. inherited lineages. They are often the bits of DNA lying between genes – as mutational snips within a gene may have a catastrophic impact on 'fitness'. The average person boasts around five million snips in their DNA.

High-throughput means that a great deal of DNA can be rapidly assessed generating large data sets in a 'do-able' time. For example, I worked with a team that repeated a 1980s biodiversity study (Lambshead, 1986: my PhD project) using the new molecular biology techniques. I originally typed 113 nematode morphological-species from the Firth of Clyde using essentially a nineteenth-century technique of extracting and 'clearing' over 10,000 specimens, mounting them on slides, and examining them under high-power microscopy; it took me three years. Our later genomic study (Fonseca *et al*) typed 182 nematode species from the same region in about 3 per cent of the time.

Clearly, I and my microscope missed some!

Haak *et al* (2015) found that the primary origin of the current indigenous human population of Britain was the culture known to historians as the Bell-Beaker phenomenon. Please note that the word indigenous or native used here is employed ecologically to mean a migrant population that arrived in the remote past such that they are embedded in the ecosystem.

In the early third millennium BC, two new pottery styles spread rapidly across Europe. One was the 'Corded Ware' culture which, from around 2,900 to 2,350 BC, stretched across northern Europe and southern Scandinavia from the Rhine to the Volga. It is associated with a large westward migration of Indo-European-speaking nomadic people from the Yamna culture of the southern Eurasian steppes (Haak *et al*, 2015).

In western and northern Europe, Corded Ware developed into the Bell-Beaker culture from about 2,800 to 2,300 BC on the continent, but not until 1,800 BC in Britain: more conservatism of an island culture or just another example of the barrier presented by seas?

Recently Olaide *et al* (2018) analysed a data set of nearly one and a quarter million overlapping snips from 400 ancient European bodies that dated from about 6,700 years ago to 2,800 years ago. They merged this data with 2,572 present-day individuals to give a picture of the origins of modern indigenous Europeans. Broadly speaking they supported earlier ideas of a northern migration of steppe-derived people into Europe.

From the point of view of this book, the key part of this large and detailed study is an analysis of the Beaker period in Britain. What Olaide *et al* (2018) reported is that 'The genetic profile of British Beaker-complex-associated individuals shows strong similarities to that of central European Beaker-complex-associated individuals.' British Beaker populations show 'large amounts of steppe-related ancestry' in complete contrast to earlier British Neolithic populations. The closest similarity of the British Beaker populations is with the similar culture in the Netherlands. The results suggest that by the Middle Bronze Age, the population turnover in Britain had been at least 90 per cent.

The British population by about 1500 BC, both male and female, was almost entirely derived from the migration of people whose ancestors had been living in Europe only one thousand years before. This really was culture change associated with migration and population turnover. As an aside, 'turnover', the replacement of one genetic population by another, is the result of one population out-reproducing the other. By itself, the data offers no clue to why one of the populations was more reproductively successful. It is worth noting that we are still not absolutely sure of the processes resulting in the grey squirrel replacing the red in Britain, despite being able to observe the event as it happens, so no assumptions should be made about why one human population replaced another in prehistory.

Strontium and oxygen stable isotope analysis on British skeletons from the Bronze Age suggests that few people moved far in their lifetimes, so we are probably looking at a slow migration and population build-up within Britain rather than an 'invasion'.

Modern Genomes

Nature, in 2015, published an important paper on 'The fine scale genetic structure of the British population' by Leslie *et al*. They analysed over two thousand samples of people from rural parts of Britain who had four grandparents born geographically close together. The logic is based on the premise that until recently rural British people tended to stay put, giving a genetic window on the past. The results are based on over half a million 'snips'. This is a large-scale, comprehensive and authoritative study.

Leslie *et al*'s results show that lowland areas of Britain comprising most of southern and central England share a single gene pool with distinct pockets in the highland areas to the north and west.

Orkney is the least like the other regions of Britain, which will surprise no one given the isolated nature of the islands and their unique history. The mainland of Britain divides into two groups: Wales and the rest. The authors conclude that 'the data suggest that the Welsh clusters represent populations that are more similar to the early post-ice-age settlers of Britain than those from elsewhere in the UK'. The Welsh cluster then subdivides into a North Wales group and a South Wales group, following the geography of the region.

The next split is between a northern cluster, consisting of northern England and Scotland, and a southern cluster, of central and southern England. The genomic split aligns with geography, rather than any putative cultural division between Anglo-Saxon Northumbria and a Brythonic/Gaelic-speaking northern region. There is something resembling a northern gene pool, centred around the Scottish lowland belt.

The last primary splits are between Cornwall and the Lowlands and between Scotland and northern England.

The modern genomic map of Britain shows no split into an 'Anglo-Saxon' group and a 'Celtic' group. Cornwall clusters with Devon which clusters with the primary lowland gene pool. The Cornish show no particular genetic affinity with the Welsh despite sharing Brythonic. Similarly, there is no particular relationship between Cumbria (Brythonic-speaking into the Middle Ages) and Wales. Cumbria clusters with Northumbria to form a northern England group that shows the strongest affinity with Scotland.

Branch lengths on the analysis give some indication of degree of difference between groups – the longer the branch, the greater the difference. The North and South Wales groups are about as distinct genetically from each other as they are to lowland England, and the genetic differences between Cornwall and Devon (aligned with the River Tamar) are comparable to, or greater than, those between northern England and Scotland.

In short, to quote Leslie *et al* (2015) 'We saw no evidence of a general "Celtic" population in non-Saxon parts of the UK. Instead, there were many distinct genetic clusters in these regions, some amongst the most different in our analyses.'

Broadly speaking this is the product of typical biogeographic processes. Agricultural humans are primarily a lowland species so a unified gene pool forms in the connected lowlands with genetic bottle-necking of populations migrating into the uplands along productive valleys. The further from the lowland pool, the more distinctive the local semi-isolated population.

When on holiday in North Wales I was struck by the fact that the fastest way to get from one valley to the next was to drive down the valley into England to traverse north-south and then drive back into Wales up the valley. Hence there is no unified Welsh gene pool.

Leslie *et al* (2015) also compared the genetic structure of Britain with a data set of 6,209 individuals from across Europe to assess shared ancestry and so try to track Anglo-Saxon migrations into Britain. This is problematic as it must be stressed that unfortunately no genetic marker is conveniently labelled Anglo-Saxon. The results one gets from genetic analysis depend on what parts of the genome one decides are representative of the migrating peoples. Leslie *et al* use complex statistical analysis to objectively identify 'chunks' of DNA that are likely to indicate Anglo-Saxon migrations; broadly speaking, a chunk of DNA that is geographically widespread across Britain probably indicates an earlier migration than one that is localised.

The first chunk, identified from German samples, they labelled GER3. If GER3 alone is used as a marker to indicate Anglo-Saxon ancestry then the Anglo-Saxons contributed about 10 per cent of the genetic inheritance of the British lowlands. However, if an additional chunk of DNA (DEN18 from samples from Denmark) is added, the estimate for the proportion of Anglo-Saxon inheritance in the Lowlands rises to 20 per cent. There is a third chunk of DNA (FRA17 – from French samples) which may show Saxon ancestry, although the relationship is now becoming tenuous. If FRA17 is included, the estimate for the proportion of Anglo-Saxon inheritance in the lowlands rises to around 50 per cent, but there is no reason to think that Anglo-Saxons migrated into Britain via France in any numbers so the use of FRA17 is problematical – it could easily be a confounding variable giving a false correlation.

Leslie *et al* (2015) concluded that 'the proportion of Anglo-Saxon ancestry in [the lowlands] is very likely to be under 50 per cent, and most likely in the range 10–40 per cent'. They also find evidence for 'significant pre-Roman but post-Mesolithic movement into SE England from the Continent'. We must always bear in mind that migration across the Channel has always gone on – in both directions.

Statistical analysis of the data can yield one further piece of evidence to test the identification of GER3 with Anglo-Saxon migrations: the timing of GER3's arrival into Britain. The GLOBETROTTER algorithm (geeks like exotic names for software: my organisation boasted a BEOWULF cluster) can be used to time the admixture of a migrant chunk of DNA into the host population. When applied to GER3 in the UK data it gives an admixture date of AD 858 with 95 per cent confidence intervals of +/- 56, i.e. around AD 800 at the earliest. This is 350 years or so too late if we conflate the genomic result with the well-established archaeological evidence for Anglo-Saxon migrations onto the island.

This anomaly could be due to: (i) an unknown variable distorting the results, a particular problem with a single data set like this without replicants (called daemonic intrusion in ecological statistics!), (ii) an incorrect generation time estimate skewing the resulting date, (iii) the date for the admixture is right but the identification with Anglo-Saxons is wrong or (iv) migration of people and admixture of genetic 'chunks' may genuinely have two different dates suggesting the two populations did not interbreed until long after the initial migration.

(i)　'Daemonic intrusion' is by definition unknown so there is no point in considering it further except to remind ourselves that it happens – and garlic fails to solve the issue.

(ii)　The calculated admixture date depends on an accurate estimation of generation time turnover in early medieval Britain: Leslie *et al* (2015) used 28 years. However, they note that if this is extended to 33 years or more, it pushes the admixture date back to the seventh century, more closely but still not precisely matching the archaeological data.

Estimating human generation times is problematical (see Langergrabber *et al*, 2012). Genetic studies commonly use quite a low generation time of 20–25 years – but generation time data from the last two or three hundred years where we have records is more like 30–32 years. The problem is compounded because humans are a sexually dimorphic species, with the generation time of men being five years or so longer than women. In theory one would need the sex ratio of the *successfully reproducing* portion of the total population for accurate estimates. Langergrabber *et al* suggest 29 years for a pre-industrial society (women 26 and men 32 years).

Leslie *et al*'s (2015) reluctance to push the generation time in their analysis much beyond 28 years is entirely sensible and conservative. There is absolutely no reason to push generation times among early medieval people up far enough to make the archaeological and genetic data sets contemporaneous – other than circular reasoning, also known as making the evidence fit the hypothesis rather than the other way around.

(iii)   A paper by Kershaw & Røyrvik (2016) suggested that the date mismatch between the archaeological and genetic data could be reconciled if it is assumed that GER3 indicates not the Anglo-Saxon migration but the later Danish migration. The dates certainly fit but the identification of GER3 as not Anglo-Saxon begs the question 'Where are the Anglo-Saxons?' If the British lowland population is derived from an assimilation of British and Scandinavian populations then why do we speak English instead of a Romantic language derived from Vulgar Latin (and/or Brythonic) or some composite language derived from Scandinavian and Latin (and/or Brythonic)? In short, the Scandinavian hypothesis raises more issues than it solves.

(iv)   The final explanation is to accept both the archaeological evidence and the analysis of Leslie *et al*'s (2015) until such time as more data or a better analysis is available. The time-gap can then only be explained by a fifth-century onwards migration of

Anglo-Saxons but with the two populations remaining more or less distinct until significant admixture starts two hundred years later at the earliest. This implies the Anglo-Saxons migrated into empty living space in Britain.

Conclusions

To sum up: (i) there is no evidence for a 'Celtic' single gene pool, just a typical association between geographic and genetic isolation, (ii) there is no evidence for Anglo-Saxon warlords leading powerful warbands into Britain exterminating the indigenous population or causing them to flee: the locals probably outnumbered the migrants at any one time, and (iii) the migrants and indigenous population may have lived in an 'empty land' with little interaction for at least two centuries.

We are still left with three questions: (i) how did the most populated part of Britain with the most sophisticated civilisation become 'empty'? (ii) why didn't the Romano-British kingdoms expand eastwards into the power vacuum to appropriate the lowlands? and (iii) how did a migration of Germanic farmers making up eventually half or less than the population so completely dominate as to result not in a blending of two cultures but the complete loss of the indigenous culture, including both language and religion?

Chapter 3

The Languages of Britain

The Common Tongue of Roman Britain

Vulgar Latin, the common speech of the inhabitants of the Dominate (the later Roman Empire), differentiated regionally and evolved into the modern European Romance languages from the seventh century onwards. The pronouncement of the third Council of Tours reinforced this process in 813 by instructing priests to preach in the local language rather than formal (archaic?) written Latin.

Language is deeply interwoven into identity concepts of ethnicity (Wallace-Hadrill, 2008). In the late Roman Republic, for example, Cicero writes that to understand Latin is the mark of a Roman citizen. Little is known about the details of the Vulgar Latin dialect spoken in Britannia, but it is a reasonable assumption that it was not that dissimilar to the version spoken in Gaul. Similarly, it is not known how far the British rural population adopted Vulgar Latin as a first language rather than their native Brythonic. Sparse evidence in the form of the written word leaves open wide differences of interpretation. However, it is noteworthy that Britain has produced fewer stone inscriptions than other provinces. Soldiers mostly commissioned the inscriptions that exist so they are found in the non-urbanised military upland zones.

Brythonic was not a written language before Romanisation so it is unlikely to leave permanent records, even by people who favoured it as their primary spoken language. Woodcock (2016) provides a good summary of the extant data.

The Bath and Uley 'curse tablets', dating from the second to the fourth century, list 178 names, split roughly 50–50 between Brythonic and Latin. Names give some clue to ethnic identity and hence favoured language, but even this is not certain: most of us know people with names derived from one ethnicity that identify with a quite different one.

In Britain, the northern and western non-Germanic regions preserved Latin as a high-status language – something like the use of French in

England after the Norman conquest – but by around 700 AD Latin was a dead language (Charles-Edwards, 2012).

The Latin in Gildas' *De excidio et conquestu Britanniae*, written in about 540 (possibly?), is replete with the language of the Latin Bible spoken by the educated, i.e. clerics, rather than ordinary people who presumably in the uplands still used Brythonic. The idea that Latin was already becoming fossilised in Britain is reinforced by the role of British Latin as a historical source used for the purification of the language on the continent in the time of Charlemagne, to distinguish it from the developing Romantic vernacular currently in use. With regard to language, 'pure' and 'unchanging' are synonymous with 'archaic'.

While it is not so surprising that the ordinary people of the upland military zones in Britain retained Brythonic throughout the lifespan of Britannia, and indeed into the future as Welsh, Cornish, Breton, Cumbric and possibly Pictish, it does raise the question over the language spoken in the lowlands both before and after the conquest.

No written Brythonic from the Roman or pre-Roman period has been discovered, except for a couple of what appear to be Roman-era curse tablets from Bath. To put it in perspective, 128 of the 130 tablets recovered are in British Vulgar Latin (Adams, 2005). Many of the authors were low on the social scale, implying that the use of Vulgar Latin was widespread – at least in the region around Bath. Tomlin (1979) lists 110 various Latin markings on tiles connected with such matters as batch numbers, signatures, and what looks like graffiti.

Tacitus in *Agricola* stated that the language of Britain was similar to Gaulish, and Gaulish appears closely related to Brythonic. British toponymic (place name) evidence from Ptolemy's *Geography* points to a Brythonic rather than Germanic origin. Indeed, about two thirds of England's rivers still have names derived from Brythonic, including the Thames.

In short, the best reconstruction that can be made from such limited evidence we have is that the native language of Britain was Brythonic but that a British form of Vulgar Latin was possibly widespread in the lowlands of the south and east that made up the heart of the Roman province.

Britain, excluding the far north, was part of Romanitas from AD 43 to around 410, some four centuries. By comparison, Caesar had conquered Gaul by 51 BC but it completely and permanently fell out of Roman control in 486 AD after the Battle of Soissons – a period of around six centuries. It hardly seems likely that those extra two hundred years should account for the difference in outcome between the two provinces, since from 455 Germanic Visigoths, Burgundians and Franks controlled much of Gaul and after 486 Merovingian Frankish kings ruled.

This brief summary shows the divergence of the fate of the former provinces of Britain and Gaul. The Franks had contact with Rome, especially the Army, over a considerable period, and Gaul slowly transformed over centuries from Roman province to medieval kingdom. The new polity was Christian, spoke a Romantic language, and had a military culture evolved from the Empire. It is unlikely that much would have been different if Syagrius (the last 'Roman' military commander in northern Gaul) had won the Battle of Soissons. Syagrius himself was assassinated, after having been handed back to Clovis by the Visigoths to whom he had fled for asylum. His family, nevertheless, prospered under the Frankish monarch, remaining wealthy landowners and enjoying titles such as Count and Abbot.

It is worth looking at another Roman frontier province before leaving this topic, Dacia. Roman Dacia only existed from AD 106 to 275, just 170 years. It was located in what is now Romania and had a population of about a million. The province was urbanised with ten cities, agriculturally productive, monetarised, and wealthy from gold and other mining products. The presence of about fifty thousand military personnel added to the province's prosperity and importance.

This all ended with the crisis of the third century which seems to have impacted Dacia early, if interpretations from coin-hoard evidence are sound. Dacia suffered from depredations from the Carpi and Goths despite Emperor Philip the Arab's victory in 247. The Goths defeated the Roman Army in 251, killing the Emperor Decius. Erection of inscribed monuments in the province fall off after 260 and Aurelian officially abandoned the province by 275.

Abandoned, in this context, probably meant withdrawing the Army and Imperial civilian administrators. It did not mean an organised evacuation of citizens or even local administrations. Roman towns continued to exist, at least for a while, but the southward pressure of barbarian migrations led to Dacia being renamed Gothia by about 295. The Romans mounted punishment raids into the ex-province, the last one led by an Emperor being the invasion by Valens in 369. The destruction of a Roman army and the death of Valens at Adrianople in 378 marked the end of direct Roman involvement in Dacia and there is little archaeological evidence for the continuation of a Roman lifestyle to any large degree (Oltean, 2007).

And yet modern Romanians speak a language derived from Vulgar Latin. Romanian contains more Latin grammatical constructs than other Romantic languages and the 2,500 words most frequently used are derived from Latin. The origins of Romanian became tied up in nineteenth-century nationalism. In particular there was a determined drive to purge the language of Slavic loan words and re-Latinise it, which may partly account for this Latin focus.

Broadly speaking, explanations for the continuation of Latin usage in Dacia after Rome withdrew fall into two camps: survival and immigration. The survival hypothesis is that the civilian population continued after withdrawal of the Roman administration, reinforced by movement of trade and people backwards and forwards across the Imperial boundary supplemented by locals being recruited into the Roman Army before returning home upon discharge. Christian liturgy would also reinforce the use of Latin. The immigration hypothesis is that immigrants from the south, which had been Roman for 500 years, emigrated north into what is modern Romania after the fall of the Western Empire.

These two hypotheses are not mutually exclusive and at the moment the issue is unresolved. However, the survival hypothesis is simpler so until evidence to the contrary emerges, parsimony suggests that it should be accepted. All of which makes the elimination of Vulgar Latin from Britannia all the more surprising.

The Influence of Brythonic on Old English

The Old English (Anglo-Saxon) spoken in post-Roman England is a West Germanic language, with grammar more like modern German than modern English. The oldest manuscripts date from around AD 650 so earlier forms of the language are conjectural. Such Latin words that are found in Old English commonly have cognates in other Germanic languages, suggesting that they entered the language as loan words before it was introduced into Britain.

In recent years, intensive analysis has focussed on finding evidence for Brythonic influence on Old English. The traditional view held that the language was almost devoid of Brythonic, although that conclusion was not universally followed. No less a figure than J.R.R. Tolkien took an opposing view. Some possible Brythonic inclusion into English has been suggested based on sentence construction. For example, Brythonic was analytic, word order rather than declensions conveys the meaning of a sentence. Old English was synthetic like Latin, case endings to words convey sentence construction rather than word order.

Middle English is more analytic (the change is known as 'drift', a term coined by Edward Sapir) and one possible explanation is that the Old English analytic was spoken by a Germanic elite while the ordinary people spoke a more mixed language, but this is speculative. For reference, Proto-Indo-European is considered synthetic, with complex grammatical conjugation and grammatical genders.

There were pockets of Brythonic speakers in what is now England until quite recently, for example the Fens in East Anglia, Cumbria and Cornwall. Brythonic influence on Middle English grammar could just as easily have occurred much later than the migration when these final Brythonic speakers were incorporated into an English identity.

The key point is that neither Brythonic nor Vulgar Latin seems to have greatly influenced Old English. There are few loan words from Brythonic and the few Latin loan words may have been in the language before the Anglo-Saxon migrations. The linguistic evidence is against Old English being created by a merger of West German dialects with either of these two languages. The primary exception is that many place names, especially those connected with topographic features or pre-Saxon settlements, are Brythonic or Brythonic-Germanic (Fleming, 2010). Brythonic examples include rivers (Thames, Avon), hills (Pennines, Malvern Hills) and forests (Arden, Wyre).

We therefore have a conundrum. There is no evidence for large scale (or indeed any) use of Germanic dialects in Britain up to it falling out of the Roman Empire, suggesting Anglo-Saxon must have been introduced afterwards. If so, why did it replace Vulgar Latin in the lowlands? If Vulgar Latin was only spoken by an elite who disappeared from the lowlands at the end of the Empire in Britain then why did not Brythonic become the language of what is now England? Why did Vulgar Latin continue as an elite language in the least Romanised parts of Britannia but not in the most Romanised and why is there no fusion of Brythonic and Germanic into a composite language?

How Roman were the British?

Romanisation of the lowlands of Britain proceeded energetically after the conquest. The Roman Army constructed some 9,000 km of roads in Britain, half being completed by the end of the first century with most of the rest constructed by the end of the second century. The British were about to be thoroughly civilised whether they liked it or not.

Romans embarked on an ambitious building programme, initially with constructions of a military nature or purpose, e.g. forts at key river crossings, legionary bases, ports, lighthouses and, of course, the roads necessary to link these military structures. Wherever the Roman Army campaigned, they built.

Within a few decades, towns (*vici*) grew up around the bases to service the needs of the military; retired soldiers established *colonia* providing a useful base and source of manpower in emergencies; and tribal capitals (*civitates*) were established in appropriate local sites in a deliberate policy of Romanisation of the British elite.

Tacitus described the process:

> '[Agricola] wanted to condition [the Britons] to peace and leisure by providing delightful distractions. He gave personal encouragement and assistance to the building of temples, markets and town-houses, he gave the sons of the aristocracy a liberal education, they became eager to speak Latin effectively and the toga was everywhere to be seen... And so they were gradually led into the demoralising vices of porticoes, baths and grand dinner parties. The naïve Britons described these things as "civilisation", when in fact they were simply part of their enslavement.'

The Romans rebuilt Londinium, Verulamium (St Albans) and Camulodunum (Colchester) after the Boudiccan revolt. By AD 80, London boasted a forum, governor's palace, basilica and amphitheatre. By the end of the century, lighthouses had been built at Dubris (Dover) to match the one at Boulogne. To the west, Fishbourne Palace was erected shortly after AD 75.

However, a general point that strikes one immediately is how little impact indigenous British people had on the Empire in a leadership role. This is puzzling because Rome was inclusive so far as ethnicity is concerned. Broadly speaking, they divided humanity into freeborn Romans, Roman slaves and freedmen – and 'the rest'.

Ethnic origin was no bar to joining the Roman elite. For example, Gallic senators, drawn from the families of elite Gallic warrior-aristocracies, took seats in the senate from the reign of Claudius only a century after the conquest of Gaul but we know of not one single British senator – ever. Similarly, we have no record of any senior British military commanders until under Constantine III, let alone British emperors. There is no obvious reason why Britain should not have supplied emperors like every other frontier province containing a substantial military presence, especially in the later Empire ruled by military dictators. As Jones (1987) notes, 'No great officer of state, no generalissimo, no high-ranking bureaucrat, can be traced back to a British origin.'

Named Roman Britons, other than client kings at the start of the conquest, only appear in the records in the late fourth century. Silvius Bonus is the only known British poet. Ausonius in 385 makes fun of the poet with a play on words implying that to be a Briton and to be 'good' (*bonus*) is a contradiction in terms.

The cleric Pelagius, apparently British born with a Brythonic name – a Graecized version of Morgan or sea-born in English – came to be infamous in the early fifth century as a heretic and so denounced by all right-thinking Romans. Jerome referred to Pelagius as 'stuffed with Scottish porridge', i.e. he was a barbarian/not really Roman. Orosius also implied Pelagius was barbaric because of a monstrously large body. Constantius III (more of him later) received similar smears – 'slow-moving glutton' – implying that because he was associated with Britain, he must be a large, greedy, dim-witted barbarian (Jones, 1987). No libel laws existed to inhibit a good insult in the Roman world so possibly one should not read too much into these comments alone, but I think they are interesting as fitting into a narrative of Briton equals barbarian.

There is another anomaly that has already been touched on. Britain, like some other peripheral provinces, lacks civilian inscriptions in stone compared to more central provinces. Jones (1987) points out, 'Latin civilian inscriptions are an important symptom of successful Romanisation and urbanisation, implying the successful assimilation of the imperial language and attainment of civic habits.' The large number of curse tablets are associated with civilians rather than the army and are uniquely British (Mattingly, 2006). This might simply be a reflection of some peculiarly British trait, the army not being British, or given that the tablets address theft, they could be telling us something about the level of lawlessness in Britain and/or the indifference of the Roman authorities to the welfare of their British subjects.

The poet Florus, in his *ambulare per Britannos* on the subject of Hadrian's visit to the island in 122, wrote he 'would not like to be Caesar, to walk among the Britons'; hardly a ringing endorsement. The 'savage Briton' had become a Roman poetic trope.

Vindolanda Tablet 164 introduces the term Brittunculi: the term is pejorative rather than affectionate. Vindolanda Tablets Online translates this word as 'wretched Britons'. We must remind ourselves that this is not a barrack-room term used by a couple of drunk *contubernales* (squaddies) relaxing in some dive in the *vicus* (urban development around a military base) but is written on a tablet by an officer assessing the military capabilities of the locals. The assessment is not flattering. These tablets are dated from between AD 92 and 103. Now, it is possible that 'Brittunculi' is indicative only of the Army's attitude to barbarous peoples in the north and that soldiers demonstrated only the highest respect for the newly urbanised *Brittones* to the south, but that seems unlikely.

In short, after three centuries of Romanisation one gets a distinct impression that educated Romans still regarded *Brittones* as semi-barbarians, unlike their close cousins from Gaul whose elite were civilised and respected citizens.

Conclusions

The traditional view explains the dominance of the English language by invasions of powerful Anglo-Saxon tribes/warlords exterminating Romano-British culture by fire and sword in the most brutal fashion. Except that (i) we have evidence for Germanic migrations not invasions and (ii) powerful Germanic warlords did invade all the other Roman

European provinces and formed Romantic-speaking kingdoms with an early adoption of Christianity. It is noteworthy that the Normans, who became the English ruling class after the 1066 invasion, left Britain with a substantial archaeological impact but (i) Norman French did not replace English although it did influence it and (ii) this tiny elite left no genetic trace that we can detect.

The Anglo-Saxon kingdoms that emerged from the collapse of Britannia show little cultural assimilation from either Latin or Brythonic.

Finally, doubts remain about the success of the Romanisation of Britain in a wider cultural sense than just language. The Roman elite, and hence the wider Roman populace, seem not to have accepted British-born Romans as equals. The indigenous people no doubt reciprocated with hostility.

Chapter 4

Conquest and Pacification

Why Rome Invaded Britain

Rome conquered Britain for reasons different from those that are the cause of most conflicts in the modern world. We are used to thinking of war in terms of competition for trade, the acquisition of resources to feed industrial civilisations, or as a clash of political ideologies. None of these were driving forces of the Roman invasion.

Briefly, the Roman Republican senatorial aristocracy competed amongst themselves for influence, glory and prestige by acquiring public offices along a hierarchical track called the *cursus honorum*. The summit of this track was to be one of the two annually elected magistrates, the consuls, and the peak of a consular career was to command the legions in a victorious military campaign. Political and military leadership were so intimately bound together that successful politicians were usually also generals.

Politicians in the Late Republic needed money, a great deal of money, to run successful political campaigns and pay their armies. Commonly this had to be borrowed. Creditors understood that successful politicians would use and abuse their political/military power to enrich themselves to pay off their debts and bribe jurors in any resulting corruption trial.

Provincial governor of Sicily, Verres, himself prosecuted for corruption by no less than Cicero in 70 BC, is infamous for supposedly insisting that a governor had to make three fortunes: one to pay back his election debts, one to bribe the jurors in his corruption trial and one for himself.

It is no doubt indicative of Roman attitudes in the Republican period that the Latin word *provincia* referred to land suitable 'for conquering' (Elliott, 2020): newly elected consuls were awarded a province and an army.

The conquests of the Second Punic War and of the Hellenistic kingdoms raised the stakes considerably. Politicians commanded armies in aggressive wars of conquest to acquire loot for personal glory and hence political power and influence. This was an era of warlords. Julius Caesar invaded Gaul and Britain to enhance his prestige, personal political influence and wealth – mostly in the form of slaves. Slave traders notoriously followed in the wake of Roman armies.

Rome inextricably intertwined political power, wealth and military glory. The first ruler of the Principate (early empire ruled by Roman aristocrats), Augustus, ended the era of the Roman civil wars with copious stores banked of all three. His successor, Tiberius, rightly enjoyed a reputation as a successful general with military glory, and as Augustus' chosen heir, acquired money and political power; but a problem arose with the third emperor, Caligula.

As Tiberius' heir, Caligula had political power and wealth but had never commanded troops in combat, let alone won the sort of military fame that would justify a Triumph – the Roman street parade that was the ultimate acknowledgement of military prowess. Caligula needed a military victory so he could be hailed *Imperator* (conqueror) as well as *Princeps* (first citizen, i.e. emperor). So the modern word 'emperor' comes from the Roman word for 'conqueror'. The humiliating stories about Caligula's supposed ineffectualness in military leadership are not unconnected with his assassination after a mere four years in power. The same pattern repeats itself with Nero, although he managed nearly fourteen years on the throne before his forced suicide.

Claudius faced the same issue, but the list of potential targets for a quick and easy military victory were limited. Expeditions across the Rhine promised little in the way of glory or loot, just drawn-out, meaningless, attritional warfare in dark forests against impoverished barbarians. Nothing of value could be gained but a great deal could be lost – as Varus discovered in the Teutoburger Wald massacre. Similarly, Crassus comprehensively demonstrated that Parthia was a tough nut to crack even if it did offer strategic targets for the Roman Army and copious potential loot to display in the victory parade. Iberia, Gaul and the north African coast were already Roman, so that left only Britain.

At this point, it is worth stopping to consider what Rome knew or believed about Britain before the conquest. The island was an anomaly in the Roman world view. To the Romans, the world consisted of three continents of roughly equal size – Europe, Asia and Africa – set in a world ocean. To be sure there were islands, but islands were small, geographically inconsequential features. Britain on the other hand was large. Indeed, there seems to have been some doubt in the Roman mind whether Britain should be classed as an island at all until the northern campaign of Agricola proved the matter beyond doubt. Germanicus' soldiers who were washed up in Britain after a great storm returned home with Odyssean tales of monsters and magical dangers at the edge of the known world.

Going beyond the known world greatly enhanced Julius Caesar's glory and prestige when he invaded the island. The senate voted the warlord a twenty-day *supplicatio* (thanksgiving) upon hearing of his first and arguably militarily-disastrous British expedition. Claudius' troops mutinied when ordered to board the transports for the invasion and something similar may be behind the bizarre stories about Caligula's aborted enterprise.

By the time of Caligula, the Roman ruling classes must have acquired substantial knowledge of southern Britain, both its geography and political structure. They understood it as a sophisticated civilisation with a hierarchy and population centres that promised both a strategic target for winning military glory and the necessary social structure to afterwards incorporate another province into the Empire, accruing yet more glory for the victorious Princeps. How much they knew about the geography and political structures in the north and west of the island is debatable.

A Quick and Easy Invasion

Aulus Plautius commanded the Roman invasion force which landed on the south coast in AD 43. Boulogne with its Roman lighthouse probably served as the main embarkation portal although the landing zones are still disputed. Richborough remains the most likely site but an additional or alternative landing in the Chichester region is not impossible. Plautius fought and won a contested river crossing in the region of the Medway Gap against a British army led by King Cunobeline's sons, Togodumnus and Caratacus of the Catuvellauni. The general pursued the British to the Thames where the army halted, waiting for Claudius to arrive and formerly receive the surrender of the British south-eastern tribes. Claudius had to be 'in at the kill' so the prestige for a successful campaign accrued to the throne rather than the generals.

Vespasian led a force into the West Country while the rest of the army advanced north and west. By AD 47, the Roman Army and its client kings controlled most of the productive lowlands ending on the Devon border to the west and south-east of a line from the Severn to the Humber. The Roman Road now called the Fosse Way runs more or less along this line from Exeter to Lincoln. The Latin for ditch is *fossa* so a fortified ditch as a border marker possibly ran along the Fosse Way before the road was built to facilitate troop deployments.

The land south-east of the Fosse way incorporated the territory of the Cantiaci, Atrebates, Durotriges, Dobunni, Catuvellauni, Iceni, and Corieltauvi. These, not at all coincidentally, were the coin-minting tribal areas of Britain enjoying a social system sufficiently sophisticated for successful incorporation into the Empire.

Caesar conquered all of Gaul in a campaign lasting from 58 BC to the Battle of Alesia in 52 BC, i.e. six years, with only a couple of additional seasons for mopping up operations. Conquering the part of Britain equivalent to Gaul took Plautius just four years. It seems probable that, with the example of the failure in Germany, the Romans never intended to rule the lands beyond the Fosse Way.

Cassius Dio wrote:

'The senate on learning of [Claudius'] achievement gave him the title of Britannicus and granted him permission to celebrate a triumph. They voted also that there should be an annual festival to commemorate the event and that two triumphal arches should be erected, one in the city and the other in Gaul, because it was from that country that he had set sail when he crossed over to Britain.'

Recalled to Rome, Plautius enjoyed an ovation in which the Emperor honoured the general by walking alongside him. The British campaign ended in decisive victory exactly as planned, much like the Coalition's triumphal entry into Bagdad just three weeks after the invasion.

A Long and Painful Pacification

One of the lessons that echoes down through history but apparently needs to be relearnt by every generation is that it is deceptively easy for the army of a sophisticated, organised nation to break into the territory of a disorganised nation of warriors but winning the resulting asymmetric conflict is far more challenging. If the Fosse Way was the Roman intended stop line then they were in for an unpleasant surprise.

The new British governor, Scapula, launched an assault against the Silures late in the campaigning season in AD 47, either as a response to Silurian raids on Roman-controlled territory or in search of the British resistance leader Caratacus who had resurfaced there. The Romans hunted down Caratacus, defeating his army in a set piece battle in the territory of the Ordovices – the tribe to the north of the Silurians. The British still failed to grasp that warriors could not defeat legions in a pitched battle, let alone a siege.

As well as campaigns in Wales, Scapula put down a rebellion by the Iceni (Norfolk) and a coup against a Roman ally in the territory of the Brigantes (northern England). More asymmetric warfare erupted in south-east Wales with heavy Roman casualties.

Meanwhile, Romanisation of the south-east started, with London, Colchester and St Albans founded.

Galba, governor from AD 52–57, was bogged down in more insurrections in Wales and northern England. With Rome now on the defensive, Nero appointed Veranius, and then Paulinus, to mount aggressive campaigns in Wales. In around AD 60, Paulinus destroyed the Druid-infested Isle of Anglesey, a centre of resistance from the British perspective but probably something resembling a 'terrorist camp' in the eyes of the Roman authorities.

This 'decisive' victory still failed to pacify Britain. Taking advantage of the absence of the Roman Army in faraway North Wales, the Iceni of East Anglia erupted in revolt once again but this time on a far larger scale. 'Boudica' destroyed Colchester, decisively defeated a detachment of the Legio IX Hispana destroying its infantry formations and forcing the legate to flee, burnt London to the ground and sacked St Albans. The death toll of Romans and Romanised British reached an estimated 70,000 or more and the whole province looked lost.

According to Suetonius,

'[Nero] thought of withdrawing the army from Britain and changed his purpose only because he was ashamed to seem to belittle the glory of his father.'

Note that the importance of 'glory' outweighed any economic or strategic advantages of abandoning Britain.

All Imperial rulers show political reluctance to retreat from territory after a defeat, and Nero, to reiterate, faced the same problem as Caligula and Claudius in that he lacked a military reputation. The lost *auctoritas* (power, authority) from withdrawal could easily mean the Emperor's immediate overthrow in a coup organised by a contemptuous military. For example, 'Lampridius' blamed Alexander Severus' timidity in trying to bribe German foes to go away rather than fight them for the Emperor's assassination by 'the swords of his own men': note, bribing barbarians was a strategically better and cheaper option than fighting them, as Tiberius wrote to Germanicus. But of course, nobody would accuse Tiberius of timidity – at least not twice.

As an aside, it is worth reminding ourselves that the first two emperors, Augustus and Tiberius, who had the respect of the army, died of old age. Of the next three, only Claudius escaped being dethroned in a coup and he bathed in the reflected glory of the conquest of Britain.

I am assuming that the scurrilous tale of the formidable Agrippina deliberately feeding the old man some dodgy mushrooms is merely gossip, although at least one modern medic, William Valente from the University of Maryland School of Medicine, pointed out that Claudius' reported symptoms did match those of muscarine poisoning. Muscarine, an alkaloid found naturally in some mushroom taxa, attacks the peripheral nervous system. Valente joked at the Seventh Annual Clinicopathologic Conference that Claudius died *de una uxore nimia* – of one too many wives.

In the event, Paulinus saved the province with his victory at the set-piece Battle of Watling Street, proving once again that warriors should stick to asymmetric warfare against a regular army.

Cerialis brought northern England under control in the campaign of AD 73: he commanded the Legio IX Hispana in the Boudiccan disaster. Frontinius finally pacified the Silures and their Welsh allies in AD 76, although Agricola had to reconquer the Ordovices once again in 78, campaigning as far as Anglesey. By my reckoning, Agricola was the fifth Roman general to conquer Wales in a single decade. In 79, Agricola thrust back into northern England and from 80 to 84 subdued Scotland.

Britain had been thoroughly conquered but it required 37 years and 9 commanders in marked contrast to the mere 8 years for Caesar's conquest of Gaul.

By the end of the century, the Roman Army had largely withdrawn to the 'Stanegate Line' – Corbridge to Carlisle. The far north of the island could not be incorporated into the Imperial system so was abandoned and any plans to invade Ireland quietly forgotten, if they ever existed.

The Size of the Roman Garrison of Britain

At this point it is worth addressing the question of the size of the Roman Army garrisoning Britain in the principate.

Strabo, writing in the reign of Augustus, noted in his *Geographia*,

'Wherefore the island would be hardly worth a garrison, for it would require at least one legion and some cavalry to enforce tribute from them; and the total expenditure for the army would be equal to the additional revenue, since if a tribute were levied, the duty must of necessity be diminished, and at the same time some dangers must be incurred if force were to be employed.'

The vital strategic military zone of the Rhine encompassed two provinces, Germania Inferior and Germania Superior. The troops there protected the wealthy province of Gaul from marauding Germanic warriors and by extension Iberia and even Italy so Rome understandably and entirely sensibly deployed substantial military assets in the region. Holder (2003) calculates for the early second century a Rhine army of no less than four legions supported by forty-six auxiliary units, of which one fifth were cavalry. This gives a theoretical manpower of close to 49,000.

Holder (2003) also estimates the Roman Army in Britain had no less than three legions and 56 auxiliary units – again around one fifth cavalry. Not only had Britannia a larger garrison then either of the strategically crucial Germania provinces, its 53,000 manpower was greater than both combined. This astonishing manpower begs the question – what were they defending against?

The population of Roman Britain in the second century is estimated at about three million (Alcock, 2011) so if we take Holder's (2003) estimate of 53,000 soldiers, then 1.8 people in every hundred in the province are soldiers. This is similar to the wartime establishment of the British Army in the early nineteenth century at the height of the Napoleonic wars, 1.6 soldiers per hundred people, but considerably more than the 'peacetime' establishment of the late eighteenth century of 0.25 soldiers for every thousand people in the population. To put these figures into some sort of perspective, the equivalent figure for modern Britain is around 0.18 per thousand, at least until the next Strategic Review (i.e. 'cuts').

Mattingly (2006) estimates a figure of 55,000 men for the Roman garrison in the second century. Elliott (2017a) notes that this represents about 12 per cent of the Imperial Army's order of battle, and all for a province that contained about 4 per cent of the land area of the Empire. How much Britain was worth as a percentage of the GDP of the Empire is probably impossible to calculate but one may reasonably doubt whether it was as much as 4 per cent given the size and riches of the trading cities of the eastern Mediterranean and the agricultural produce of North Africa.

It is interesting that legionaries make up about 45 per cent of the Rhine garrison but only 31 per cent in Britain. The proportion of auxiliary units to legions in Britain increased from the first to the second century and by the middle of the latter period numbered some seventy units, the highest for any province in the Empire. This implies serious security issues in the province that were not improving with time. Legions supplied core heavy infantry for set-piece battles so the high proportion of more flexible auxiliary units suggests that the problem was constant widespread insurrection rather than large invading forces offering pitched battle.

As discussed earlier, Strabo took the view that Britain was not worth occupying because the tribute obtainable would hardly pay for the upkeep of the necessary garrison of 'one legion and some cavalry'. Even if Britain turned out to be larger and more valuable than Strabo assumed, one struggles to see how it was worth the pay of three legions and quite a few squadrons of cavalry, not to mention auxiliary infantry.

Conclusions

Rome invaded and stayed in Britain for political rather than strategic or economic reasons, not least because the Emperor's very life depended on maintaining *dignitas* (prestige, respect) and *auctoritas* – these words do not easily translate into modern English. The island proved easy to invade and the British easy to defeat in set piece battles but they fiercely resisted pacification.

The unexpected size of the Roman garrison in Britain suggests something more resembling an army of occupation in hostile territory than a mere security force to keep order – especially as there was little obvious external threat to the province at the time other than the northern frontier. The heavy emphasis on auxiliary units implies actions small in scale but widespread and occurring simultaneously, i.e. continual insurrection and banditry.

Romanisation of Britain could be held down and exploited but resisted incorporation into the Empire as a functioning Roman province, and in that sense Romanisation failed. The evidence suggests continuing disdain on the part of the conquerors and sullen resentment on the part of the conquered, a simmering hostility that all too easily flared into outright violence.

Chapter 5

Romanisation and Conflict

Londinium, Boom Town of the Roman 'Wild West'

The Principate is the name given to the first phase of the Roman Empire from its founding by Augustus to the crisis of the third century, 27 BC to AD 284. The title *princeps*, the 'first citizen' ('first among equals' conveys the idea in modern English), that was conferred on Augustus and his successors disguised the reality of monarchical powers. Kings were anathema to Romans, hence the political sleight of hand.

Londinium formed the largest and most important urban centre in Roman Britain and in some respects the story of Londinium is the story of Roman Britain. The summary presented here is largely taken from a recent comprehensive overview by Hingley (2018) and the references therein.

The official status of the city is unclear. It probably started simply as a *vicus*, a civilian settlement serving the needs of the local fort on the Thames crossing, but may have been elevated to a *colonia*, (a city of Roman citizens and veteran legionaries) in AD 120. It seems to have served as a provincial capital and its official renaming as 'Augusta' in the fourth century presumably reflected that status, although clearly the locals ignored the name change as the name Londinium survived into the modern world.

Londinium stood on low hills on the north bank of the Thames between two rivers, the Fleet and the Lorteburn, straddling a third – the Walbrook. Opposite the Walbrook, what is now Southwark consisted of a north and south island, providing 'stepping stones' across the Thames.

Watling Street, connecting the channel ports with the military zones to the north and west, crossed the Thames at this point and connected there with an east-west road. Numerous streams feeding the Walbrook supplied plentiful drinking water to the city from the spring line.

Early on in the Roman invasion, someone constructed a waterfront and Londinium became an important inland port. It is possible the first bridge was also built at this time. By the time of the burning of the city in the Boudiccan revolt, it had a population approaching ten thousand and grew into a booming mercantile centre as well as a military supply base.

The rebuilding of Londinium started immediately and haphazardly after the revolt. Evidence, including tablets from the city itself and Vindolanda, suggests the presence of senior officials based in Londinium, possibly including the Provincial Governor. Public buildings arose, including an amphitheatre, forum-basilica, temples and bath houses. By the early second century, a substantial building, possibly a *praetorium* (governor's palace), appears in London and a *mansio* (a sort of ancient motel for individuals travelling on official business) constructed in Southwark.

Interestingly, no urban defences protected Londinium or small British towns. Only *colonia* were surrounded by ditches. One might assume that the city was considered safe or unimportant. Well, Londinium was hardly unimportant so that explanation is unpersuasive. However, defensive ditches and walls are 'force multipliers' having no defensive value in themselves except to multiply the strength of any defenders versus an attacking army so perhaps there was simply insufficient military presence in London to make it worth constructing fortifications. *Colonia* by definition included military veterans who would be quite capable of defending ditches amongst the resident population.

The archaeological evidence suggests that late first-century London was a mercantile boom town, not unlike a midwestern American town reached by the railroad.

Boom towns need resources, in particular building material. Industrial scale quarrying in the upper Medway Valley began soon after the invasion (Elliot, 2017b), increasing throughout the first and second centuries. The five quarries investigated by Elliott (2017b) are enormous: Dean Street 356,400m^2, Quarry Wood 215,000m^2, Allington 61,600m^2, Boughton Monchelsea 54,600m^2, and Teston 35,830m^2.

The Medway Valley contains evidence of a substantial Roman presence, including four villas, other stone buildings, roads and iron workings. Ships like the Blackfriars vessel, dated to AD 140, carried stone the 127 km down the canalised Medway and along the Thames to London. Elliott (2017b) estimates the return journey could be made in four days.

He further suggests that industry on this scale would have required the military to organise and control the large numbers of slaves, prisoners of war and criminals worked to death as labourers – assuming that forced labour was employed. The likely candidate is the *Classis Britannica* which operated the Blackfriars-type ships.

In classical civilisation, an individual or family demonstrated their power and prestige by paying for the erection of public monuments. Some might be purely decorative or of civilian utility but it is quite possible that town defences might also come into this category. This will be discussed further in a later section.

In short, the evidence is that Rome invested substantial resources into Britain, or at least the lowlands, to create a fully functioning Roman province from the ground up with nothing already in place. There is no suggestion that Britannia would be treated differently to any other province.

The 'Long Hot Summers' of the Early 120s

Trajan's widow, Plotina, conveniently produced adoption papers that made Hadrian Emperor after Trajan's death. At the time, Hadrian was away from Rome fighting the perennial Jewish revolt so Hadrian's praetorian prefect represented the new Emperor in Rome. He quickly executed four senators without trial, suggesting Hadrian's accession was not greeted with universal enthusiasm by the Roman elite. Casual executions of aristocrats tended to sour relations between throne and senate so were not lightly embarked upon, especially at the start of an emperor's reign when his seat was insecure. At Hadrian's accession, rebellion flared in Britain, Judaea, Egypt, Mauretania and on the Danube. Indeed, some of Trajan's conquests had to be abandoned (Hoffman, 2017).

How much the shaky legitimacy of Hadrian's rule influenced events in Britain is unknown and probably unknowable, but the *Historia Augusta* records that 'the Britons could not be kept under Roman control'. Cornelius Fronto reported a British Hadrianic war, suggesting that Roman casualties in the province were on the same scale as the Jewish 'Bar Kokhba' revolt of AD 132. Roman casualties in the Jewish war included the almost complete destruction of the Legio XXII Deiotariana and heavy mauling of the Legio X Fretensis. It has also been suggested that the Legio IX Hispana may have been destroyed in this war, but more about the famous 'Ninth' later.

Other evidence for serious unrest in Britain exists. An AD 119 coin showing the word Britannia may have been celebrating a Roman military victory in the province. Then, there is the *expeditio Britannica*, where military detachments from the VII Gemina, VIII Augusta and XXII Primigenia were dispatched to the province under the command of T Pontius Sabinus. The word *expeditio* in this context implies a military campaign. The exact date of this visit is contentious but Breeze (2003) suggests a late date, and hence war, of 124 or 125. This date would match the issue of the 124/5 and 125/6 'nike' coins by the Alexandrian mint. These coins refer to warfare somewhere unknown in the Empire, and Britain is a candidate as no other contemporaneous war is known.

Hadrian visited Britain in AD 122 and work started on his Wall immediately or even earlier (Graafstal, 2018). Legio VI Victrix is traditionally assumed to have arrived in Britain in 122 from Lower Germany accompanying the Emperor and the new governor Platorius Nepos as a replacement for the Legio IX Hispana.

Breeze (2003) offers evidence that there was a pause in the construction in 124 plus or minus a year and he links this to the *expeditio Britannica*. In his model, work restarted on the Wall in 126/7. Essentially, Breeze (2003) suggests two separate wars in Britain, in around 118 and 124 (see also Mattingly, 2006). The construction of the Wall implies a strategic requirement to separate off the population within the Empire from their uncontrolled countrymen in the north, presumably to impede coordinated insurrection. The Emperor's visit in 122, as well as the building of the Wall, could be seen a response to the first war but possibly triggering the second.

One might reasonably assume that the second 124 insurrection postulated by Breeze (2003) might also be in the north were it not for a recent analysis by Perring (2017) on the fires in Hadrianic London. Elliott (2021) calls this work 'ground-breaking', and with good reason.

Perring's conclusion of a major insurrection in London shortly after Hadrian's visit to the province rests on three major strands of evidence: a reanalysis of the fires, the Walbrook skulls, and the construction of the Cripplegate fort.

Archaeologists have known since the 1940s that substantial parts of Londinium burnt down during the reign of Hadrian. The exact date is difficult to specify other than the 120s (Perring, 2017, Hingley, 2018, Elliott, 2021).

The scale of destruction matched that inflicted in the earlier Boudiccan revolt but the question remains whether 'the fire' (i) an artefact, the friction of time causing us to conflate a number of completely independent events, (ii) a single conflagration caused by one accidental event or (iii) or the deliberate razing of the city by insurrectionists?

Perring (2017) presents compelling evidence that the Hadrianic fire was a single conflagration. Post-war excavations show contiguous fire damage over 65 hectares covering almost all of Londinium north of the Thames. These areas include the residential, mercantile and governmental buildings. Two areas noticeably escaped destruction – Southwark and the Upper Walbrook valley – both industrial zones (Elliott, 2021).

Of course, cities do burn down purely accidentally – London in 1666 and Rome in AD 64 are examples – so a city-wide accidental fire must stand as the parsimonious null-hypothesis, but Perring (2017) compiles evidence to suggest the fire was not accidental. A fire starts at a single point and then spreads downwind along buildings packed tight together, halting at natural firebreaks in areas of low-density occupation.

The Hadrianic disaster does not follow this pattern. The fire in individual buildings appears to have started at the front, suggesting arsonists moving along the street torching buildings as they went (although Gilkes pers. comm. pointed out to me that streets can act as wind tunnels giving similar patterns). The Walbrook failed to act as a firebreak with fires occurring in both east and west Londinium.

Valuables seem to have been stripped from the properties before they caught fire. The natural action of property owners or their agents would be to salvage what they could as the fire spread, but equally looters would steal any mobile valuables before firing the property. One interesting feature was discovered in a house on Watling Street – sheets of bronze recording the granting of Roman citizenship fused together in the heat of the blaze (Elliott, 2021). A citizenship diploma represented an easily retrieved artefact of great value to the owner and his heirs, but only scrap metal value to looters. This is only a single datum point so perhaps we shouldn't read too much into it but it is suggestive when added to the weight of evidence.

Turning to the evidence of the crania recovered from the Upper Walbrook and tributaries, the number of skulls recorded is astonishing – currently around 300. More turn up with every digging activity, most recently from Crossrail construction work. It is known that many more skulls have been found over the years and discarded without archaeological examination. Elliott (2021) notes that to put this figure of 300 into perspective, only 29 skulls are recorded from all other places within the boundaries of Londinium.

Nearly all the skulls are male from men of military age, 28–35. Stratigraphic dating puts their deposition within a time band from AD 120 to 160. Many of the skulls show signs of violence to a degree that implies executions or damage resulting from the heads being displayed on a trophy rack. As an aside, Gauls were commonly recruited into Roman auxiliary units especially in the cavalry and Gauls had headhunting traditions (Elliott, 2021).

Perring (2017) points out that in Roman culture denial of proper burial was an exceptional punishment reserved for those who challenged public and social order, particularly those considered guilty of treason and betrayal, so might be considered a form of *damnatio memoriae* (a modern term despite meaning in Latin 'expunged from the record'). Unburied dead represented a spiritual danger that could be purged by disposing of the remains in running water associated with the boundaries of the city.

In short, the skulls probably represent the remains of men not just considered mere enemies killed in honourable battle or those executed for civilian crimes but of people executed en masse for treason.

A slightly larger than life bronze head of the Emperor Hadrian pulled out of the Thames just below London bridge in 1834 had been hacked from a statue that presumably graced some public place such as the Londinium forum. This artefact is now exhibited in the British Museum. The statue had likely been commissioned to celebrate the Emperor's visit to Londinium in 122. So how did an emperor's head get hacked off a statue and thrown in the river? The forum and basilica were burned in the great Hadrianic conflagration but the head shows no sign of fire damage so presumably the statue was vandalized before the fire, which narrows the time frame considerably. Desecrating an imperial statue and disposing of the head in flowing water is not unknown in the Roman world (Perring, 2017). This act presumably has a magical significance not unlike the disposal of real heads in the same way.

There is historical precedent. The decapitated bronze head from a Roman statue found in the River Alde at Rendham in Suffolk is identified with that of Nero, ripped from the Temple of Claudius in Colchester by Boudicca's British rebels (Crummy, 1997).

Perring's (2017) final strand of evidence is the building of the Cripplegate fort. The army similarly built a fort in London after the Boudiccan disaster but it had been dismantled by the second century. Urban garrisons were rare in the Empire except for a handful of strategically important cities. The Cripplegate fort measured 200 by 215 metres so Perring (2017) estimates it housed at least 1,350 cavalry and infantry. This is far too big to simply accommodate the bodyguard and military aides of the governor. The fort fits awkwardly into the pre-existing road network suggesting it was a rushed, unplanned construction. Like the post-Boudiccan revolt fort, the Cripplegate fort had a short span of use. There is no evidence of military occupation after AD 165.

Hingley (2018) concludes, 'The fort at Cripplegate was constructed soon after [the Hadrianic fire] and this could suggest as in the case of the earlier (Boudiccan) burning of AD 60/61 that the fire was the result of a deliberate attempt to destroy the city after which a military unit was stationed at Londinium to supervise the reconstruction.'

Perring's evidence for the looting and burning of Londinium in the mid-120s is persuasive but questions remain. Firstly, was this part of a wider war? Could Londinium be collateral damage in the putting down of a military coup? No evidence has been presented for similar impacts on any nearby Roman urban settlements. While accepting that absence of evidence is shaky ground for evidence of absence, surely some collateral damage somewhere other than London would have surfaced by now if there had been extensive military action? The Boudiccan revolt, arguably full-scale war with two set-piece battles, left archaeological evidence at London, Colchester and St Albans.

Localised insurrection and public disorder of an extreme nature is a more likely possibility. The obvious question that naturally follows is who were the insurrectionists? It seems unlikely that enough British warriors could be assembled in the south-east into a force capable of sacking a Roman city. Where would they come from? Why were they not intercepted by Roman military units? The other possibility is that the insurrectionists came primarily from within the Roman system itself.

The Lost Legion of Britain

In 1954, Rosemary Sutcliffe wrote a highly popular children's novel about the destruction of the Legio IX Hispana in a war against the northern Brittunculi in the early second century which was televised. The loss of this legion in Britain at around this time was widely accepted. The Ninth had a long association with Britain, forming part of the original invasion force and being badly mauled by Boudicca's warriors.

The Ninth campaigned against the Brigantes (northern England) and formed part of Agricola's army in the conquest of what is now Scotland. Once again, the legion endured an unhappy experience at the hands of British warriors who, according to Tacitus, 'burst upon them as they were terrified in their sleep'. The unit only recovered its morale after being rescued by the cavalry.

The last record we have of the Ninth places them in York in 108 where they left inscriptions recording their work on the legionary fortress, but after this – silence!

Perceived historical wisdom later rowed back on acceptance of the legion's destruction in Britain: Dando-Collins (2010) somewhat tongue in cheek suggests academic embarrassment at the commercial success of a children's novel may be a factor. However, there is evidence such as inscriptions including a silver-plated bronze locket belonging to a senior officer that places the legion on the Rhine after 120. But do these records refer to the whole legion or simply a detachment?

Dando-Collins (2010) points out that several auxiliary units were transferred from Britain to the Rhine in 113 but had returned by 120. He also notes that five auxiliary units based in Britain also disappear at around the same time as the Ninth: the Alla Agrippiana Miniatra, 1st Nervorium, 2nd Vasconum CR, 4th Delmatarum and the 5th Raetorum.

The pendulum of opinion on the fate of the legion is swinging back to a British explanation and, possibly as a result, Sutcliffe's story has been reworked for a modern audience by Jeremy Brook in the 2011 film *Eagle* which was directed by Kevin McDonald.

Dando-Collins also (2010) takes the Sutcliffe option as the most probable scenario. He suggests that the legion and its associated auxiliaries were destroyed in the north in AD 122 or shortly after. He offers as evidence the fact that Lucius Norvius Crispinus Martialis Saturninus (who survived) served as a tribune in the unit from 121.

Elliott (2021), while agreeing a northern disaster is the most likely scenario, offers an additional variant on the Sutcliffe option. He suggests that the Ninth deployed down Ermine Street from York after 122 to deal with a crisis in London and was destroyed in the south. The problem with this scenario is that it is difficult to envisage an indigenous force in or around London at this time capable of annihilating a legion.

Elliott (2021) offers a third most intriguing scenario – that the Ninth were not the victims of the London insurgency but the protagonists. Legions had mutinied before. For example, the XXI Rapax, V Alaudae, I Germanica and XX Valeria Victrix mutinied in AD 14 after the death of Augustus. They murdered tribunes, threw their bodies in the Rhine, looted civilian property, and planned to sack and burn the city of Cologne. This mutiny started not on the Rhine but in Pannonia. The Pannonian legions involved were the VIII Augusta, XV Apollinaris – and the IX Hispana (Wilkes, 1963).

Dando-Collins (2010) makes an interesting observation that Saturninus, the Ninth's tribune who we know survived, was never employed by Hadrian again. His next command had to wait until Antonius Pius became Emperor.

I wonder why the Romans left no record of the fate of the Ninth. They were not usually shy about recording losses in battle, including the destruction of whole legions in catastrophic defeats, cf the Teutoburger Wald. The complete silence on the fate of the Ninth smacks, to me anyway, of a collective *damnatio memoriae*.

Although Latin, *damnatio memoriae* is a modern phrase referring to the time-honoured practice of officialdom erasing problematic individuals or events from the record – if necessary, by rewriting history. The practice is as old as human civilisation and is not entirely unknown in the modern world, especially in Marxist dictatorships. George Orwell's protagonist Winston Smith, in his novel *1984*, works at Ingsoc's Ministry of Truth, rewriting the historical records to fit the latest political requirements.

In Rome, the practice tended to be applied to traitors and particularly heinous criminals, usually involving political or religious offences.

So, for what it is worth I offer my own complete speculation as to the fate of the Ninth. I suggest the Legio IX Hispana was officially forgotten because it collectively committed treason by mutinying as Elliott (2021) speculates, probably killing many of its officers. Clearly it didn't rebel in the north and then march south to sack London while ignoring York and all the property on the way, so in this scenario it must have mutinied in the vicinity of Londinium itself. The cause of the mutiny was presumably connected with the legion's relocation. So what might have been the primary motive behind such extreme dissatisfaction?

The Ninth had been in Britain for the best part of a century and many of the men probably had roots in the province such as unofficial wives and other dependants. They and their comrades had fought and died in Britain most probably quite recently in the northern war just prior to 120 and no doubt expected to retire in Britain on grants of land in familiar countryside among relatives and old comrades. There was no reason to base a legion in the south-east in the mid-120s so the Ninth if they had marched south were just passing through on their way overseas, possibly to the Middle East. This might have been enough to induce a mutiny as rumours of a transfer out of the island among the rank and file became cast iron certainty with their arrival at the channel ports.

The second Jewish War (the Kitos War) finished in AD 117 leaving a volatile situation in the Eastern Mediterranean. Hadrian stripped Trajan's successful general, Lusius Quietus (after whom the Kitos War is named), of command as soon as the war ended and was believed to have ordered his murder in 118. It is possible that Hadrian's decision to abandon Trajan's conquests was unpopular with the legions – the Emperor Severus Alexander was assassinated by his soldiers for something similar – and the Emperor may have wished to have politically reliable troops from the west on hand in case of unrest among the eastern legions.

In this model the Ninth, or at least part of it, rebelled, sacked London and was eliminated by loyal forces. The authorities executed surviving rebels and disbanded what was left of the legion, striking it from the records.

For what it is worth, chemical evidence from just a single London Wall skull exists. Genetic analysis suggests his mother probably came from the Eastern Mediterranean region and that he had black hair and brown eyes. Stable isotope evidence supports the conclusion that he was not born in Britain (Elliott, 2021).

In London, the rioters attacked the citizens' town houses, the warehouses and the public buildings because that was where the portable loot was, and because mutineers and runaway slaves tend to attack symbols of authority. Cologne came within a whisker of a similar fate in AD 14.

A legion's mutiny makes a good story so must be treated with a degree of caution. However, the scenario does fit the limited facts available.

Urban Fortifications

Esmonde Cleary (2003) lists four ways that urban defences in Britain stand out compared to other western provinces: (i) Britain has more urban defences by the end of the Principate, (ii) there are many earthwork fortifications, (iii) many small towns are fortified and (iv) British stone walls enclose larger areas.

The first point to address is to consider the function of defences in the Roman Empire. Until recently this question would have seemed ridiculous to historians. One fortified a site to defend it against a real or perceived threat. But since the 1960s historians have shown a marked reluctance to acknowledge the role of violence in society. Brown (1971) was one of the first to view late Roman history through the lenses of anthropology and sociology. In this world picture the Western Empire does not so much 'fall' as 'change'.

Our interpretation of the past tends to reflect contemporaneous preconceptions, and Western society in the second half of the twentieth century enjoyed increases in wealth, comfort and security to a level unknown to their forebears. As I write in the early twenty-first century, confidence in the continuation of these desirable circumstances is eroding which is possibly why we now see the re-emergence of interest in the fall of civilisations. In particular when it comes to the collapse of the western Empire, value-free concepts of 'transition' are being challenged by more robust considerations of the consequences of system collapse (Ward Perkins, 2005).

With regard to fortifications in Roman Britain, Esmonde Cleary (2003) concludes, 'Urban defences in the West were much more to do with urban status and civic ambition than with defence.' He further suggests 'applying this [concept] to towns and villages in Roman Britain... give them a more satisfactory context than "wars and rumours of wars".' In the same paper, Cleary reminds us that there is never one simple cause for any historical phenomenon.

Halsall (2013) notes,

'Spending private money on [high-status] projects brought important political rewards. It might bring success in the competition to control the curia (town council) of the civitas. The curia was responsible for tax collection... an important source of patronage. Success here... [would]...be a platform for advancement on a broader political stage, the acquisition of Roman citizenship, and perhaps even promotion to the higher orders of Roman society.'

Rational self-interest could provide motivation for seemingly expensive altruism. A modern analogy might be a successful but not socially well-connected British entrepreneur funding charitable works and donating to political parties with the expectation of receiving a knighthood and subsequent entry to 'the establishment' with all the business and social advantages that would bring.

If we consider fortifications to have a military function then we must bear in mind, as already mentioned, that they are force-multipliers for defending troops only. Walls and ditches have value only when manned by a garrison. This applies as much to modern fortifications such as bunkers and minefields as ancient or medieval city walls.

Military engineering can serve multiple functions; status and military usage are not mutually exclusive. In modern history, battleships performed valuable service 'showing the flag' in foreign ports but nations that built powerful battle fleets also intended them to fight. One can imagine a wall being built for its military function and then faced in beautifully cut stone to demonstrate the status of the community.

I find it difficult to understand why earthworks should be constructed as a sign of status in Roman Britain but not in other western provinces. Earthworks in particular, being cheap and buildable by unskilled labour, suggest a purely functional utility. The expensive monumental stone gateways contemporary with, or even predating, urban earthworks offer no particular military advantage and must be considered to be high-status constructions.

It is also unclear why the Romans fortified more small towns in Britain. Did small towns in Britain really have more 'civic pride' than their continental neighbours? Esmonde Cleary (2003) notes that British small towns were larger both in terms of population and economy and so possibly more important. Being 'more important' in itself doesn't differentiate between 'status' and military utility as the cause of fortification. It merely suggests that British towns had more resources to deploy.

If, as I argue here, earthworks had a military function then we have to address the question of what they could defend against? Even manned, they would provide little protection against Roman army units or even against hypothetical (in lowland Britain) armies of barbarians. Earthworks would be of value against organised banditry so their early construction in Britain and the large areas protected imply levels of social instability not troubling equivalent towns on the continent.

Describing the fortifications of Britannia is beyond the scope of this book but a few representative examples will be discussed.

There is no convincing evidence that Londinium was protected by walls or earthworks before the construction of the city wall at the end of the second century (Hingley, 2018). Given Londinium's status within Britannia this seems odd. The city certainly possessed many high-status buildings, some abandoned in 160 possibly because of the Antoine plague that ravaged the Empire (Perring, 2011, 2015): temples were erected at this time, possibly to curry the favour of the Gods during the crisis.

The large Cripplegate Fort built after the Hadrianic conflagration would have served Londinium's military protection requirements and it is significant that the fort was abandoned when the city walls were constructed, the north and west walls of the fort being incorporated into the city defences. This suggests that the city walls served a primarily military function and were a direct response to the Hadrianic disaster.

Londinium's walls were more than 3 km long, along the landward boundary of the city, enclosing the largest urban centre in Britain. The wall was 2.5 to 3 m wide and an estimated 6 m high. Towers lined the wall's inner face. This was the largest construction in Roman Britain: an expensive project and one not lightly undertaken. The open waterfront suggests no waterborne enemy threatened and that London was an important port needing unimpeded access to the water.

The legionary fortress at Camulodunum became Colonia Victricensis – a planned urban centre for retired army veterans given plots of surrounding farming land confiscated from the locals.

Tacitus writes,

'The settlers drove the Trinobantes [local tribe] from their homes and land, and called them prisoners and slaves. The troops encouraged the settlers' outrages, since their own way of behaving was the same and they looked forward to similar licence for themselves.'

The area affected might have been considerable, causing great hardship among the local people. Ominously, repurposing the site involved removing defences. Major high-status buildings and monuments rapidly sprang up, notably the massive Temple of Claudius, a monumental arched gate where the London road entered the city, and a statue to the goddess Victory – high status constructions that did not involve fortification.

Rome immediately rebuilt Colchester after the Boudiccan destruction but took the precaution of constructing a 2.8 km long, 2.4 m thick, city wall, probably the first in Britain. It is difficult to see this as anything other than a primarily military project (Crummy, 1997).

The fate of the western monumental arch is interesting as it involves a direct conflict between military functionality and status display. The new city walls directly abutted the original arch causing a defensive weak point. Flanking towers could not be built and troops could probably not walk across the top of the gate. From a purely military perspective the arch should have been demolished. That it was not shows that ceremonial displays of status were still of equal importance.

Coastal Defence

Much of the archaeological evidence of Roman coastal defences in Britain have been eroded by the sea so we can only work with what is left. Imperial coastal defence initially rested on the *Classis Britannica* based first at Richborough then, by the second century, at Dover. Construction of a new fort started in around 130 (in Britain – Boulogne was the main fleet base). From Boulogne and Dover, the fleet controlled the narrow seas, probably using civilian ports as necessary.

Coastal defences in the form of forts, fortlets and watchtowers, constructed along the north-east coast south of Hadrian's Wall in the Hadrianic period, probably guarded against sea-raiders from northern Britain slipping around the land defences (Pearson, 2002). The fleet operating from South Shields and civilian ports probably served the same function on the north east coast, although no evidence of their presence remains.

The Severan period saw major changes in the east coast of Britain's coastal defences. The fort at the eastern end of Hadrian's Wall at South Shields was remodelled as a primary supply depot for the invasion of Scotland (Pearson, 2002). Around this time construction of the first Saxon Shore forts began. Reece (1997) questions whether the Roman Army undertook construction of fortifications solely to meet military requirements. Even in modern times the maxim that an idle soldier is a problem waiting to happen holds good – hence the interest in the British army at one time in painting coal white 'to prevent theft' (J. Southerland, *Evening Standard*, 4 September 2014). Given the reputation of the Roman Army in Britain for disciplinary issues, keeping them busy no doubt paid off – or at least stopped them marching on Rome.

Reece (1997) suggests that in the early third century the army repaired the defences on the northern and Welsh borders before working on urban defences and finally the Saxon Shore forts. Presumably some military use accrued from this work or the troops could simply have been employed more cheaply digging holes and filling them in again – given the short supply of coal and white paint in Roman Britain. Assuming there was a military function, the order of construction tells us something about the threats to Roman Britain at this time – other than from the army itself. Barbarians on the fringes were the biggest threat, followed by internal violence within the province with coastal defences on the eastern coast coming last.

Various details about the Saxon Shore forts are still matters of academic dispute, but Brancaster, Caister and Reculver are thought to be early third century. Examination of the forts' location against contemporary coastlines leads Pearson (2002) to conclude that they were positioned in 'sheltered tidal environments that lay close to, but not directly on, the open sea' – in other words excellent harbour locations for pre-industrial wooden sailing ships. The forts provided protected anchorages, but were they guarding against pirates coming in off the sea or 'bandits' operating from within Britain – or both? Gilkes (pers. comm.) suggested to me that the heavily walled forts might have offered strongpoints to police and tax 'unofficial' ship-borne trade banned from other ports.

Walls And Usurpers

Strategically, Hadrian's Wall separated the local people in northern Britannia from their countrymen to the south. The intention was the civilisation or at least pacification of the Britunculi to the south.

Pausanias, in his *Graecae descriptio* makes an infuriatingly throwaway reference to Britain that is difficult to interpret with certainty:

> '[Antoninus] deprived the Brigantes in Britain of most of their territory, because they too (besides the Moors in North Africa) had entered on a war of aggression by invading the Genourian part, [inhabited by] subjects of the Romans.'

Genourian is not mentioned elsewhere. It is not clear exactly when this might have happened or even if Pausanias literally meant the Brigantes tribe in northern England or was using the term generically to mean 'British'. Assuming there was some sort of rebellion, it might be dated to 140–142 when Lollius Urbicus advanced north into Scotland and constructed the Antoine Wall. The implication being that British north of Hadrian's Wall had attacked the lands to the south and had been 'deprived of their territory' by the advance north.

Another possibility is 154–155 when Antoninus celebrated a victory with coin issues and the army rebuilt a number of forts in northern England. The implication here is that the Brigantes south of Hadrian's Wall rebelled, possibly in response to withdrawal of troops from northern England to man the new far northern fortifications (Hind, 1977). The Antonine Wall was abandoned in 162 but the Roman Army still maintained a presence in Scotland. For example, the fort at Newstead, Trimontium, was still occupied until AD 180.

Breeze (2006) suggests that the motive for the advance north and the building of the Antonine Wall may have been as much political as military. Antoninus became Emperor without military honours to his name so he had the same political problem as Caligula and Claudius. He needed a cheap, easy, but politically impressive military success, and once again victory over the barbarous British supplied it. After the advance, Antoninus was proclaimed Imperator for the first and only time of his career.

In Breeze's model, military necessity forced the abandonment of the Antonine Wall. The retreat back to Hadrian's Wall shortened the line releasing men for use elsewhere. The land between the walls was of no economic or strategic use, to the Empire at least, and the Antonine Wall had outlasted its political value; after two decades, Antoninus' position on the throne was secure.

A recent paper by Hanson (2020) gives a somewhat different perspective, noting that a major construction rethink delayed completion of the Antoine Wall. The builders added a series of secondary forts, some of which replaced fortlets in the original design. Gillam first suggested that the Antonine Wall original design planned for forts every 11.8 km as on Hadrian's Wall. The Antonine Wall as completed boasts forts 2.4 to 5.8 km apart, with 80 per cent being less than 4 km.

To put this in perspective, forts along the German *limes* in the Taunus and Wetterau are around 9 km apart, at Oldenwald 5 to 15 km apart, 11 km in Western Raetia, and 10 to 25 km in Dacia. Hanson notes this makes the Antonine Wall one of the most heavily defended frontier zones in the Empire. He also draws attention to an apparently Roman-destroyed broch at Leckie, some 15 km north of the Antonine Wall. All of this points to serious resistance possibly because the Antonine Wall created a 'hard border' that split the Dumnonii.

The 'military necessity' causing the retreat back to Hadrian's Wall after two decades might have been precipitated partly by endless insurrection in the area as well as other military and political requirements.

The construction of Hadrian's Wall and associated structures, their abandonment, construction of the Antonine Wall, and then the abandonment of the latter and repair of Hadrian's wall might seem to modern eyes to be a colossal waste of resources that would horrify even a civil servant, but that is to project our preoccupations and economic realities onto Rome. They did not think in economic terms, and in any case, the building work was undertaken by the Army. The Army had to be fed and its soldiers paid irrespective of whatever it was doing. The Roman Army in Britain proved itself ill-disciplined and generally truculent so it is worth reminding ourselves once again that a soldier kept fully occupied expending surplus energy on building walls is likely to present less of a problem to his superiors.

Moving on by a couple of decades, Dio Cassius records,

'When the tribes in the island, passing beyond the wall that separated them from the Roman legions, proceeded to commit many outrages and cut down a general, together with the soldiers that he had, Commodius was seized with fear and sent Marcellus Ulpius against them. This man, who was temperate and frugal and always followed strict military rules in regard to food and all other details when he was at war, became in course of time haughty and arrogant. He was conspicuously incorruptible in the matter of bribes, but was not of a pleasant or kindly nature... This was the kind of man Marcellus was, who inflicted great damage upon the barbarians in Britain.'

According to Dio Cassius,

'The greatest conflict [of Commodius' reign] was the one in Britain.'

Archaeological evidence bears this out with destruction of forts at Halton, Chester, Rudchester and Corbridge along the route of Dere Street (Elliott, 2018). Marcellus prosecuted war north of the wall until about 184, despite indiscipline and near mutiny in the Roman Army of Britain. A strong suspicion exists that the martinet Marcellus did not so much complete the war as leave one jump ahead of a lynch mob.

Dio Cassius takes up the utterly bizarre story:

'The soldiers in Britain chose Priscus... to be emperor; but he declined, saying: I am no more an emperor than you are soldiers. The lieutenants in Britain, accordingly, having been rebuked for their insubordination,... now chose out of their number fifteen hundred javelin men and sent them into Italy. These men had already drawn near to Rome without encountering any resistance, when Commodius met them and asked: "What is the meaning of this, soldiers? What is your purpose in coming?"... "We are here because Perennis is plotting against you and plans to make his son emperor."'

Perennis was Commodius' praetorian prefect, an important position. Nevertheless, the Emperor handed him, with his wife, sister and sons, over to the army to be executed.

We will never uncover the political undercurrents in play but what is clear is that the Roman Army in Britain was out of control. According to the *Historia Augusta* another disciplinarian, Pertinax, was sent to restore order with limited success:

'He did suppress a mutiny against himself in Britain, but in so doing he came into great danger; for in a mutiny of a legion he was almost killed, and indeed was left among the slain... [Pertinax] petitioned to be excused from his governorship, saying that the legions were hostile to him because he had been strict in his discipline.'

Matters in Britain came to a head with the assassination of the Emperor Commodius in 192, precipitating the 'Year of the Five Emperors'. Pertinax succeeded to the throne but was murdered by the Praetorian Guard after just three months. He is associated with the villa at Lullingstone in Kent where a bust of the Emperor was officially slighted by minor but deliberate damage to the face. Government employees (such as myself!) will recognise some cautious Roman official doing his minimal duty by slighting the bust but not exceeding said duty or showing undue enthusiasm for the task; after all, Britain was a long way from Rome and the chap who gave the order might have already been deposed and replaced by someone more sympathetic to the previous incumbent.

The Guard auctioned the throne to Julianus who was almost immediately eliminated by Septimius Severus (who was pro-Pertinax thereby justifying our unknown British official's caution). However, the new Emperor faced pretenders in the form of the governors of Syria, Pescennius Niger, and Britain, Clodius Albinus. Albinus' legacy is discussed further in Chapter 7.

The Empire never solved the problem of succession. Severus had no more moral right to rule than any general with substantial military support. With its huge army and isolated position, Britain always risked generating usurpers.

However, the pattern of events that followed was unusual. Severus and Niger fought it out until the pretender was eliminated in battle in 194, but Albinus simply formed a truce with Severus and remained in Britain as a junior colleague of the new Emperor. Indeed, it is possible that Severus encouraged Albinus' accession to ensure stability.

Whatever the truth of their relationship, the accord between Albinus and Severus ended in 195, Severus initiating hostilities. Albinus crossed in to Gaul with the best part of three legions and a large force of auxiliaries. He assumed the full rank of Emperor, setting up a mint in Lyon to pay his men. The two emperors met in battle at Lugundum in 197 with Severus victorious. Dio Cassius claims 300,000 troops were involved in the slaughter. Ancient writers notoriously over-egged battle estimates but we can assume this was a large engagement.

A Roman general with the benefit of a large army seizing the purple was not in any way unique to Britain but Albinus' behaviour was unusual in that he seemed content to rule a mini 'British' empire. His later campaign must have had a severe impact on the army in Britain both in terms of (i) numbers, many of those who left would never return, (ii) quality, the troops who left with Albinus would have been amongst the most experienced and reliable, and (iii) morale, their candidate for the throne lost.

The Expeditio Felicissima Britannica

Septimius Severus' great expedition north of Hadrian's Wall is described in detail by Elliott (2018), so only such points relevant to the thrust of this book are discussed here.

All was not well in Britain even after the elimination of Albinus. Tribes north of the Wall coalesced into two larger confederations according to Dio Cassius (formation of larger units tended to occur in 'barbarians' living adjacent to the Empire's borders for various social and economic reasons) the Maeatae either side of the Antonine Wall and the Caledonians to their north. Deforestation in this period indicates a rising population.

In 207 the new governor of Britannia, Senecio, reported new problems in the north as justification for reinforcement: Herodian gives a lurid account of barbarians 'overrunning the country, looting and destroying virtually everything on the island'. Such an event might provoke the personal intervention of the Emperor even to such a remote location, but Herodian is a far from reliable source.

The northern forts do seem to have been understaffed and rebuilding of military infrastructure was underway. Possibly questions remained concerning the reliability of the army in Britain. Some later writers refer to a 'rebellion' rather than a barbarian incursion, perhaps provoking the construction of the London city wall at around this time. Possibly the campaign was all about legacy, an aging emperor's one last bid for fame. Glory, as ever, was to be found in Britain.

Severus planned a massive campaign and launched the invasion of Scotland in 209. All the old problems of fighting barbarians resurfaced. The Maeatae and Caledonians lived in dispersed settlements that offered no strategic target for the Roman Army, so the enemy could not be forced into a set-piece battle. Dio and Herodian describe grinding guerrilla warfare over inhospitable terrain. Small warbands ambushed Roman columns and detachments only to slip away when resistance stiffened. A modern example would be the experience of the British Army's various Afghan adventures. Inevitably the Romans took losses which is not to say that they lost these low intensity battles. The American Army lost few if any battles in Vietnam. As Elliott (2018) points out, the passage of Roman armies no doubt devastated the local agricultural economy, possibly doing more long-term damage than direct combat.

The 209 campaign ended with a negotiated Roman victory, the British conceding territory – Elliott (2018) speculates this was the land between the two walls – and the Roman Army withdrew into winter quarters.

The Maeatae rebelled again in 210, presumably wiping out the Roman garrisons in the forts to the north of Hadrian's Wall. Severus' response was bleak. According to Dio Cassius he ordered the army to commit genocide using a quote from Homer: 'The whole people must be wiped out of existence, with none to shed a tear for them, leaving no trace.'

As no major problems surfaced in the north for eighty years, it seems the army succeeded.

Conclusions

After Agricola's campaign ended in 84, the Roman civil and military leaders must have considered the island well and truly pacified. They invested heavily in creating grandiose infrastructure and the industry to support it. And yet, within one generation they faced war in the north and insurrection in the south. If the reconstruction here is correct then the sources of civil unrest that were to plague the province had already reared their ugly heads in the early first century – namely, attacks by hostile British tribesman outside Roman control and rebellion from within the British province. Indiscipline and mutiny within the army and the temptation for a general commanding such a large force to rebel (the two are not unlinked) also created problems for Rome.

Despite enormous and expensive attempts at Romanisation, Britain was still unstable at the end of the second century requiring a large garrison to maintain security. This overlarge military force, isolated as it was across the 'world ocean', in many ways added to the very instability it was intended to suppress.

Chapter 6

Climate Change and Rome

The Impact of Climate Change

The crisis of the third century nominally dated from AD 235 to 284 uncovered a series of fault lines in the Roman Empire that came disturbingly close to tumbling the whole structure. The Empire split into three and was ruled by a succession of short-reigning warlords, the so-called barrack emperors.

The primary lesson from evolutionary biology is that all complex systems ultimately fail. Either they evolve into something new or they cease to exist. Any system has fault lines that are tolerable in favourable conditions but become exposed when the outer environment turns unfavourable.

Complex systems rarely fail because of any single factor unless it is overwhelmingly destructive. Normally, collapse requires a series of hits at different processes. For example, in evolutionary biology the classic example is the extinction of the North American heath hen – a subspecies of the greater prairie chicken. Hit one was the vulnerability of the bird to predation by newly arrived European settlers to the point where it was exterminated on the American mainland. Efforts were made to protect a breeding colony on Martha's Island which was successful for some decades, before a series of simultaneous blows any of which would have been survivable on its own: (i) a fire on the breeding grounds, (ii) a succession of unusually cold winters on the island, (iii) unusual numbers of goshawks, (iv) sexual imbalance and, finally, (v) disease spread from poultry.

Note that hunting by humans ended long before the bird's final extinction but was nevertheless the forcing environmental change that led to its demise. Once hunting had made the hen vulnerable by limiting its numbers and geographic distribution then bad luck in the form of fire and bad winters coupled with inherent weaknesses such as vulnerability to goshawks and poultry disease finished it off.

Climate change in the third century put the Roman Empire into stress. This was the first hit exposing fault lines. The impact of climate change on populations outside the Empire and their migratory response was a second hit that can be classed under bad luck. Finally, exposure of internal weaknesses in Roman political and economic systems struck further blows. The Empire survived by evolving into something new, the Dominate, but the changes had serious implications for Roman Britain.

Climate is a major forcing process that precipitates other impacts on preindustrial societies, especially through impact on agriculture. Broadly speaking, for the Roman Empire a warm climate was favourable and cold unfavourable. Similarly, high precipitation was good and low precipitation bad. The ideal is stability or a gently warming climate with slowly increasing precipitation.

Problems arise when either or both of these processes downturn. Agricultural production declines causing starvation. Starvation lowers the capacity of human immune systems to cope with disease so plague epidemics run wild. The death and incapacity rate climbs, further decreasing agricultural output causing more disease and death. Societal dislocation follows because the ruling class lose their authority to govern, their 'magic'. Revolution, mutinies, and insurgencies cause violence and disruption, further impeding agriculture and accelerating the process.

Populations attempt to migrate from badly hit regions, bringing war, disruption and disease; when peoples go on the move, they carry disease organisms that include strains to which the populations in the path of the migration have no resistance. Opposition to the migrants sparks conflicts which inevitably amplify social and economic disruption, greater losses in agricultural output, and... so on.

Agriculturally marginal areas suffer first so the pattern of migration tends to be from these regions into agriculturally richer lands. Pre-industrial empires grow in agriculturally rich regions that produce the greatest quantity of people, the most important resource to such economies. Migration in a climate downturn politically involves movement of 'barbarians' from the fringes into the 'civilised' imperial centres. In ancient societies in Europe, these processes spur migration from (i) highlands to lowlands, (ii) north to south and (iii) from east to west.

When the climate takes a downturn the Four Horsemen ride out – and they always ride together.

The Four Horsemen

Since the early 1980s there has been intensive study of the science of climate, driven by concerns about rapid anthropogenically-linked climate change. An important component of this research has been into past climates since by understanding the processes causing historical change science can hope to derive models to investigate future possibilities. These studies are inevitably multi-disciplinary often involving multiple research teams from various nations.

The types of data assembled include tree-ring series, ice cores, fluctuations in solar radiation, lake sediments, cave mineral deposits, written records and archaeology. Tree rings give the best resolution and information about historical climates. For the period and area we are interested in the most comprehensive dendrodata comes from north-west Europe.

There are climates that are more favourable to creating a civilisation and climates that are less so, but it is climate change and instability that poses the greatest challenge. The faster the change the greater the impact. In particular, macro-droughts lasting over decades present a lethal threat to preindustrial agriculture-based civilisations where the bulk of the population is involved in food production. Drought has been linked to collapse of a number of agrarian societies, including the Akkadian Empire and Old Kingdom of Egypt, twenty-second century BC (Watanabe *et al*, 2019), Mayan Empire, ninth century AD (Evans *et al*, 2018) and Khmer Empire, fourteenth and fifteenth centuries AD (Buckley, 2010).

Pre-industrial societies lacked refrigeration, canning, insecticides etc so had limited capability to store food surpluses when compared to the modern world. They also had a problem moving food in bulk from an area of surplus to a place suffering famine. Only ships could move such material in quantity. Transporting food using muscle power is a thankless task other than over short distances as the muscle itself requires continuous fuelling by the food carried. A modern analogy is the multi-stage space rocket where fuel is burnt to transport fuel. The powerful Saturn V heavy lift vehicle weighed 2,800 tonnes, mostly fuel, to lift a payload of a mere 43.5 tonnes to the moon.

The North Atlantic Oscillation (see later section) is the strongest source of large-scale climate variability in Western Europe. The eastern lands exhibit more complex patterns, being also influenced by other systems, including even the Pacific El Niño Southern Oscillation.

The three centuries from around 100 BC to AD 200 mark the rise of Rome from the dominant Mediterranean state to a 'global' empire. Exceptional climate stability characterizes these centuries, often called the Roman Optimum. In particular, two primary climatic 'forcing factors', solar energy and available water, both show 'unusual stability' (McCormick *et al*, 2012).

A recent paper by Harper & McCormick (2018) analyses the various data available to reconstruct the climate of the Roman Empire. Solar radiation changes may be assessed by radionuclides such as beryllium 10 (^{10}Be) and our old friend carbon 14 (^{14}C) that are created from nitrogen and oxygen by cosmic rays passing thr,ough the heliosphere. This process is inversely correlated with solar energy so accumulation of these isotopes acts as a proxy measure of solar activity – after appropriate and quite complicated adjustment for various biases. The two isotopes used together reinforce the accuracy of the signal as their fate when deposited on the surface is quite different: ^{10}Be can be found in ice cores while ^{14}C enters the organic carbon cycle and ends up in trees.

Generally, the radionuclides show strong and stable solar activity between about 300 BC to AD 600, but when the Roman period is examined at a finer scale ^{14}C suggests solar activity downturned in the early second, and, especially, mid-third and mid-fifth centuries. The fourth century shows a return to a high level of solar activity. ^{10}Be analysis from ice cores is broadly similar suggesting a clear early second century decline, a 'notable' drop in the mid-third century and a 'dramatic' increase in the early part of the fourth (Harper & McCormick, 2018).

Ice cores also record volcanic activity and Greenland cores show only low to moderate eruptions across the Roman period until a cluster of strong activity in early AD 536, causing the 'Late Antique Little Ice Age' (LALIA). Further events occurred in 540 and 547, suspiciously coinciding with the first bubonic plague pandemic in the region in AD 541 – the horsemen ride together.

Analysis of European glaciers shows a slow retreat from around 500 BC but advance once more in the second half of the third century AD. The ice retreats through the fourth century but glaciers expand rapidly during the fifth until the LALIA.

Cave and lake deposit analysis is less clear but does not contradict the general trends shown above (Harper & McCormick, 2018). However, the data so far obtained reminds us that the overall climate of the Roman Empire and surrounding districts consisted of an accumulation of regional microclimates which do not necessarily show identical patterns.

The Climate of Northern Europe during the Republic and Principate

Long term oak tree-ring data from France and Germany allows us to recreate the climate of the Roman north western provinces. Temperature falls rapidly by 2⁰C towards the middle of the fourth century BC, precipitation following a similar pattern, causing rapid climate deterioration.

Greek historian Diodorus Siculus recorded a key migratory event in Roman history at this time:

'At the same time when Dionysius lay at the siege of Rhegium [386 BC], the Gauls who lay beyond the Alps passed over those straits with a numerous army, and possessed themselves of all the country between the Apennine hills and the Alps.'

Celtic tribes from north of the Alps moved across the mountains south into what became known as Cisalpine Gaul in northern Italy. Around 390 BC a Gallic warband led by Brennus routed the Roman Army at the Battle of Allia and sacked Rome itself.

Both rainfall and temperature recovered quite quickly, temperature remaining reasonably stable and precipitation gently increasing for the next three hundred years. This was the Roman Republic's period of expansion. Rome secured Italy, southern Europe and western North Africa with the defeat of the Samnites by 290 BC, Etruscans and Gauls by 283 BC (Battle of Lake Vadimo), Pyrrhus and Taranto by 272 BC, Carthage by 201 BC, Seleucia by 188 BC, Macedonia by 167 BC, and the Germanic Cimbri in 101 BC.

It is noteworthy that Roman successes depended less on military genius (see the Battle of Arausio for a breathtaking display of Roman military incompetence) and more on its ability to raise new armies after defeat until it wore down opponents. The Second Punic War demonstrates the point: never was there a better contender for a 'battle without a morrow' that failed to win a war than Cannae. The Roman political system underpinned this resilience, but even so, Rome would not have triumphed over so many dangerous adversaries without the advantage of favourable climatic conditions producing the food surpluses and concomitant population surpluses needed to raise new armies.

The next climate deterioration with an abrupt drop in precipitation and temperature starts in the first half of the first century BC, bottoming out at around 50 BC. The downturn is particularly deep, especially the drop in temperature. This period is marked by the 'Social War' between Rome and its Italian allies, 91 BC, Sulla's civil wars, 88 and 83 BC, rebellion in Iberia, 80 BC, and the Spartacus slave rebellion, 73 BC. Throughout history climate deterioration heralds internal unrest.

Julius Caesar was elected Consul in 59 BC, in an election involving astonishing corruption even by Roman standards. Caesar was deeply in debt and open to prosecution at the end of his one-year term. He arranged to be granted the governorship of transalpine Gaul (southern France) for an unusual five years. As governor he (i) was immune to prosecution, (ii) could gouge enough money out of the poor benighted provincials to pay off his debts and (iii) win glory in some successful military campaign, given that transalpine Gaul was bordered by lands occupied by unstable tribal groups.

Successfully achieving point (i) Caesar immediately exploited events to tackle points (ii) and (iii). He takes up the story in his *Commentarii de Bello Gallico*:

> 'When [the Helvetii] thought that they were at length prepared for this undertaking, they set fire to all their towns, in number about twelve – to their villages about four hundred – and to the private dwellings that remained; they burned up all the corn, except what they intended to carry with them; that after destroying the hope of a return home, they might be the more ready for undergoing all dangers.'

Helvetii territory lay in Switzerland. An agrarian society farming marginal highlands is among the first to suffer in declining climatic conditions, thus provoking the migration Caesar describes. 328 years earlier, tribes faced with similar challenges migrated south but the new military power of Rome made that route impassable. Lands to the west offered an alternative, with the opportunity to displace a weaker Celtic tribe. The Helvetii migration would take them through Roman territory or that of Roman-allied tribes and would inevitably cause disruption and instability. Caesar had his plausible *casus belli*, igniting a series of campaigns leading to the conquest of Gaul and Rome's first foray into Britain.

Apart from a drop in temperature for a short period circa AD 160, apparently caused by changes in the NAO (Drake, 2017), northern Europe enjoyed a reasonably stable climate for the next two hundred and fifty years. The Principate expanded and consolidated during this Roman Optimum Period. However, precipitation levels fell starting in around AD 200, joined by temperature after AD 250. The climate deterioration reached a trough in the early fourth century. Rainfall levels started to recover immediately, followed by temperature at the start of the fifth century.

The period 235 to 284 is known as the crisis of the third century when the Empire came close to dissolution. It was a time of migration south into the Empire from the Barbaricum, political instability, economic crisis and plague.

Migrations out of Northern Europe and the North Atlantic Oscillation (NAO)

The NAO is the gradient between a permanent low-pressure system over Iceland (the Icelandic Low) and a permanent high-pressure system over the Azores (the Azores High) which controls the direction and strength of westerly winds into Europe. It is represented as a positive/negative index. A positive index, NAO+, indicates a larger pressure difference than normal, a negative index, NAO-, the converse.

Research on current climate processes (Visbeck *et al*, 2001) show that the NAO index correlates most closely with weather conditions in Europe across Scandinavia, the British Isles, northern France, central Europe north of the Alps and the Baltic, i.e. northern Europe. NAO+ gives stronger than normal westerlies resulting in colder and drier weather in the Mediterranean regions (i.e. unfavourable agricultural conditions) but warmer and wetter weather in northern Europe, i.e. conditions more favourable to agriculture. Such conditions provide no temptation for northern tribes to migrate south.

NAO- causes reverse patterns with unfavourable climate conditions in northern Europe. NAO negative also correlates with migration from northern Europe into the south (Drake, 2017), the migration of the Cimbri being a case in point.

According to Strabo's *Geographica*,

> 'As for the Cimbri, some things that are told about them are incorrect and others are extremely improbable. For instance, one could not accept such a reason for their having become a wandering and piratical folk as this that while they were dwelling on a peninsula they were driven out of their habitations by a great flood-tide.'

Strabo died in AD 24 with the *Geographica* unfinished so the quote above was written shortly before this date. Ptolemy, in his *Geographia* (circa AD 150) identified the Cymbric peninsula as Jutland. The Cimbri appear in Noricum in 113 BC, so must have started their migration at least a year or two, and possibly a decade or two, before this date.

Drake (2017), using a mathematical technique called Bayesian change point analysis, identified a major NAO shift with a minimum at 150 BC that is likely to have caused a drought in Scandinavia lasting years or even decades. The NAO lay between NAO-0 and NAO-1 from 200 to 100 BC. Strabo was right to dismiss rumours of a flood: drought forced the Cimbri out of their homelands.

From 100 BC to circa AD 180 the NAO index was relatively stable and above NAO+1, but Drake (2017) found a drought, albeit less serious and of shorter duration than that of 150, starting in circa AD 180 with a minimum of NAO-0.5 in 190. This was the period of the Marcomannic Wars named after the Germanic tribe of the Marcomanni although other tribes such as the Quadi and the Lazyges (Sarmatians) were involved. Up to 166, the Marcomanni and Quadi had coexisted fairly amicably alongside the Empire, but this was to change.

Goths migrated south-east out of their homeland in northern Poland starting a chain reaction that washed up on the north-eastern Roman *limes* along the Rhine and Danube. Many peoples were involved but the Marcomanni and Quadi won a major victory over the legions at the Battle of Carnuntum in 170. Roman losses estimated at 20,000 men give some idea of the scale of the Germanic incursion. The Marcomanni crossed the Alps into Italy, sacking Opitergium (Oderzo) and besieging the city of Aquileia. Rome launched a major series of military campaigns, assisted by political divide and rule tactics, to restore the situation and pacify the tribes across the *limes*.

What the Romans saw as invasions, the Germanic tribes experienced as migrations fleeing disasters – hunger, social breakdown, war and disease. An analogy is the 'invasion' of the Delta by the Sea Peoples at the end of the Bronze Age. Egyptian monuments depict carts carrying women and children, not an invading army. Whole peoples only undergo the privations of mass migration to escape worse catastrophe back home.

Rome enjoyed an advantage in that the very climatic condition that set the tribes into motion and degraded their military power favoured Mediterranean agriculture enhancing the Empire's ability to recruit healthy soldiers and provide for their logistical needs. Climate change caused by reduction in solar activity was an exception to this happy state of affairs because it hit agricultural production in the Empire as well as in the territory of the northern tribes. Rome therefore faced migrations while itself under climate strain. Hence the crisis of the third century.

The Climate of Roman Britain in the Principate

West *et al* recently (2019) produced a comprehensive analysis of the impact of the NAO on Britain using modern data from 1899 to 2015. They found that generally a positive NAO index was associated with high rainfall and a negative NAO index was associated with low rainfall, with the effect being more pronounced in winter.

Regional breakdown of the data revealed a clear north and west – south and east divide, or to put it another way, uplands and lowlands. In both zones in winter the general trend described above held true but was more pronounced in the north and west. The pattern shifted noticeably in summer in the south and east, reversing so that a positive NAO index was associated with dry weather and a negative index with wetter conditions.

A reasonable assumption is that the unusual NAO index-rainfall correlation for the southern and eastern lowlands of modern Britain was equally true in the Roman period, at least until such time as we have evidence to the contrary. Conversely, the upland areas of Britain, particularly in Scotland, would have been badly affected by NAO indexes of less than 1.

However, overlaying the NAO pattern onto northern Britain shows no particular association between low NAO indexes and military activity on the frontier. Military conflict is recorded for 118–124 (Hadrianic War), 150? (Antoninian War), 180 (Commodian War), and 209 (Severan War). The picture is more one of frequent low-level aggression until Severus' strategy of genocide.

Conclusions

Declining solar activity in the mid third century directly impacted the whole Roman Empire through agricultural decline exacerbating problems caused by tribal migrations linked to conditions in northern Europe. However, no evidence exists to suggest that NAO- played any part in the social instability that plagued Britannia.

Chapter 7

Crisis in the Third Century

Rome's Socio-Economic Fault Lines

A perfect climatological storm hit the Roman Empire in the third century. Firstly, starting in around AD 200 precipitation levels in northern Europe fell, joined by a drop in temperature after AD 250, triggering barbarian migrations southward. Secondly, solar activity downturned notably in the mid third century impacting agriculture in all Eurasia, including the Empire.

Agricultural downturn in an ancient agrarian society causes starvation, inevitably closely followed by disease and social friction. A downward spiral rotates as starvation, disease and unrest further reduce agricultural production. Central government suffers difficulties recruiting, supplying and paying troops as both manpower supply and the taxation base deteriorate. Any system in this situation does not float gently down to some new sustainable population level but plunges below it as the impacts caused by the initial problems fuel further deterioration. Evolutionary great extinctions or ecological collapses show similar patterns.

Desperate barbarians crashing frontiers whose defence was depleted by manpower reductions, taxation falls, and withdrawal of troops for internal security, added to the disaster inflicted on the Empire. The Fourth Horseman, War, joined his brothers.

As argued earlier, no system fails for a single reason. Generally, an overwhelming disruptor puts the system under pressure revealing internal problems manageable in a more favourable environment. Climatological change reducing agricultural production stands as the overwhelming disruptor for the crisis of the third century.

I now wish to turn to Rome's socio-economic weaknesses exposed by the downturn.

The Roman Empire suffered from a major impediment in that it had no constitutional way of removing an incompetent leader and, more importantly, no constitutional way of selecting a new one. The problem has its origins at the very start of the Roman Republic. Originally Rome was ruled by non-hereditary kings nominated by the senate and elected by the curiate assembly, i.e. the citizens.

After the formation of the Republic, 'king' became a dirty word in Rome and monarchic government unacceptable. The Roman Republic enjoyed a classic 'balanced' city state constitution where oligarchic magistrates were elected by 'the people' for limited periods. Consul, the most senior position, was held by two individuals chosen from the senate. Their roles included political and religious functions as well as supreme military leadership in the field. This joint role of political and military leader worked acceptably when the army was simply citizens in arms fighting local wars within a short distance of Rome, but the tradition haunted the Republic as the frontiers of the state expanded.

Roman slaves referred to their owners as *dominus*, so, when applied unofficially to the person of the emperor, the term embraced toadyism of stomach-turning magnitude. *Dominus* first became adopted as an official title under Aurelian (AD 270–275) and signified a shift from rule of the state by aristocratic 'politician' emperors to rule by whichever warlord controlled the bulk of the army.

In the Principate, Roman senators still enjoyed substantial status, as demonstrated by the value still placed on the office of consul. In the Republic, the two consuls took the role of heads of state in both political and military roles. In the Principate, an emperor filled this position but senators still enjoyed political power and the consulate opened the door to important positions such as proconsul – governor of a senatorial province.

All metaphorical roads led to Rome in the Principate and, in theory at least, emperors ruled from Rome with the support and authority of the senate. In practice, relationships between senators and emperors rarely proved harmonious, starting almost from the Empire's formation with Tiberius, the second Emperor. From Caligula onwards, senate-emperor interactions often became outright poisonous. Indeed, it is often near impossible to disentangle fact from fiction in emperors' lives as history was written by aristocrats who left no stone unturned in their efforts to blacken the emperors' characters, Caligula being a case in point. The tensions arose not because the traditional aristocracy disapproved of the system as such but because of traditional Roman aristocratic ambitions.

Patriarchs of important families saw no reason why they should not enjoy the power and prestige of being *princeps* rather than the obviously inadequate chap from a 'Johnny-come-lately' family currently sitting on the throne.

In modern terms, the Dominate was a straightforward military dictatorship. Emperors spent their time with the army, usually on the frontiers, and the capital of the Empire became wherever the field army currently pitched their tents. A large professional bureaucracy appointed directly by the emperor administrated the state: traditional Roman magistracies such as praetor or consul became irrelevant. Civilian administrators adopted military dress, although with separate lines of command from the military.

Rome's success was built on three supports. The first, the army, happily absorbed equipment and tactics from other peoples and melded them into new efficient military machines to win battles and campaigns. The second, the need for politicians to win military glory to enhance the *auctoritas* (authority, prestige, 'clout') and *dignitas* (dignity, prestige, reputation, social position) needed for political success, made the state highly aggressive. Roman politicians tended to get their retaliation in first to chase military glory. Finally, Rome was unique among ancient republics in that it extended Roman citizenship to people living in and citizens of other communities, massively increasing Rome's military manpower pool. Rome could lose battles and absorb losses that were unsustainable to Carthage or the Hellenistic kingdoms.

Success meant wars overseas requiring soldiers to be under arms for extended periods. The citizen-farmer militia transformed into a professional army. Technically, the senate raised taxes and paid soldiers' salaries in the name of the Roman People, but over time professional soldiers relied more and more on loot from successful campaigns and grants of money and land (*praemia*) on retirement. Loot depended on successful invasion and conquest – aggression that may or may not have been in the interests of the state as a whole – and the political clout of the army's general to arrange appropriate distribution of land. In short, soldiers started to look to their generals for rewards rather than the senate and showed loyalty to their general rather than some abstract state.

The generals themselves received much of the loot, making them exceedingly rich and powerful. Rising inequality was destabilising in itself in the ancient world (Levitt, 2019) but the Roman elite social structure gave it a pernicious twist. Legitimately appointed politician-generals transformed into power-seizing warlords. Political rivalry inevitably generated military confrontation and the Roman civil wars. Equally inevitably, attrition whittled away the warlords until only one remained.

The winner, Julius Caesar, then faced an insoluble problem. He ruled Rome as sole autocrat but no constitutional position existed to legitimise this position, certainly not kingship. Eventually he settled for transforming the constitutional magisterial office known as Dictator from a temporary emergency appointment made by the senate into a life appointment (made by himself).

Caesar's resulting assassination solved nothing, resulting in a new round of civil wars because the constitution was no longer fit for purpose. The next last man standing, Augustus, devised a cunning plan to achieve one-man autocratic rule while superficially restoring the old Republic. He devised the princeps principle where everyone pretended that he was merely first among equals. The senate voted him a ragbag of powers and constitutional positions but his real power was his wealth and control of the army.

The problem was that the powers of the princeps were personal and could not be inherited. No constitutional position of Emperor existed. The current emperor could nod towards a successor but couldn't appoint one. The death of any emperor always threatened another round of civil wars if more than one general in command of an army and with enough political clout fancied a tilt at the purple. For example, the enforced suicide of the last of the Julio-Claudians in AD 69 led to the Year of the Four Emperors, the murder of Commodius in 193 gave the year of the Five Emperors, and the assassination of Maximinus in 238 the Year of the Six Emperors.

While it is a truism that any successful state relies on coercion to keep unruly citizens in line, it is equally true that the acceptance of rulers by the mass of the ruled depends on legitimacy. In essence this is magic, a social conjuring trick. Legitimacy can be conferred by a variety of factors including religion (appointed by God), honourable ancestors (born to rule), democratic selection (mandate of the people), but most of all by effectiveness (the system works).

A disastrous failure destroys the 'magic' of the ruling class so stripping them of legitimacy: God has abandoned us, the election was fraudulent, etc. The pressures of The Crisis stripped away any pretence of constitutional legitimacy or senatorial approval for the appointment of emperors. From now on, power rested solely on naked military might and the ruthlessness to employ it. The parallel in the modern world is found amongst leadership contests in narco-gangs.

It is not too far a stretch to say that the primary function of a Roman army became to defeat other Roman armies in order to keep their man, their paymaster, in power. The formation of centralised field armies in the Dominate around the body of the emperor should be seen more in this light than of some strategic response to barbarian invasions such as modern concepts like 'defence in depth'.

The other major fault line that afflicted the Principate was that of a trading empire with no concept of economics. The Greek word οίκονόμος, from which we derive 'economics', actually meant something like 'household management' (Finley, 1973). Our modern concept of national economies and monetary policy traces back no further than Adam Smith (1776).

Bang (2008), in a seminal work, concludes that the Roman economy was qualitatively different from any state in the modern world. Comparison with modern Third World economies is in his view unhelpful as they are modern, differing in degree but not in substance from first world economies. He argues that the Roman economy was a bazaar rather like the economy of the Moghul Empire. Trade relationships were personal and interregional trade was not about specialisation but about the needs of the state itself – which in Rome meant the needs of the army.

Ancient states had no interest in regulating or promoting trade. Personal status drove decisions by the tiny elite who controlled the ancient world, not economic expansion. Finley points to a letter from Pliny where he discusses borrowing money to buy land. At no point does any discussion of deriving income from the land come into the debate. Buying the land is an end in itself to enhance *dignitas*, not an investment.

Bang's model of little or no market integration across the Empire has been challenged in recent years. For example, analysis of tableware distribution suggests that markets (at least for tableware in the eastern Mediterranean) were integrated and hence subject to supply and demand market economics (Brughmans & Poblome, 2016), so this is still a contentious issue.

Political and social upheaval inevitably cuts long distance trade because of lack of security for goods in transport and the inability to enforce honest dealing through a shared legal system. The Empire breaking into three independent components exacerbated these effects. How much diminution of interregional trade harmed the economy of the Empire during the Crisis depends on whether the bazaar or efficient market more accurately describes such trade. Dislocation of a bazaar would have far less impact on the economy generally than dislocation of an efficient free market.

Money came in two forms: precious metal and 'fiat money'. The earliest coins were simply small pieces of bullion stamped by a trusted state mint to guarantee the quantity of the precious metal within. Fiat money has no commodity value in itself but is accepted as a medium of exchange because it is underwritten by a stable trusted state.

The Principate used a gold aureus coin and a silver denarius with a fixed ratio of value between the two. The silver denarius started to be debased (i.e. base metal mixed in with the silver to make up the weight) from Nero onwards. Debasement continued until the denarius became fiat, but maintained its value because it was underwritten by its relationship with the gold aureus. Septimius Severus severely debased the denarius. Elagabalus demanded that taxes be paid in gold – as far as the state was concerned the 'silver' coinage had no value.

Strangely, no persuasive evidence exists that debasement of the currency caused hyperinflation, as might appear axiomatic to the modern mind (Butcher, 2015, Rathbone, 1996). Indeed, high inflation occurred in Egypt in the early fourth century – after the crisis. Given that much ink remains to flow under academic bridges on the fundamental structure of the Roman economy, trying to identify inflationary processes rapidly degenerates into pet theories.

As far as Britain is concerned, the crisis caused a shortage of coinage leading to local production of poorly made copies (Elliott, 2018). This is interesting because it suggests that a widespread monetary economy already existed within the province.

Warfare in the late Roman Republic more than paid its own way in loot, mostly in the form of treasure, slaves and indemnities paid by the losing state. Territories acquired became long term sources of useful revenue, especially the rich cities of the east. The senate allocated an army and a province to a new consul; 'province' literally in Latin meant 'for conquering' (Elliott, 2020). This happy state of affairs ended with the Principate. Wars against barbarians generated little in the way of loot but soldiers still required paying.

In the Republic, the senate raised armies to fight specific campaigns and paid off the troops when it was over. The Empire permanently stationed professional troops along the long borders, troops that had to be paid whether they were needed or not, just like an insurance policy. The Empire adopted perimeter defence because slow communications made it impossible to intercept barbarian raiders from central positions: by the time a messenger arrived at some central point to report a raid the barbarians would be legging it back over the border with the loot.

Political necessity demanded that the Emperor be seen to protect imperial possessions. Possessions had owners, often important owners who might start to wonder whether an emperor 'was sound' if too much of their portable property disappeared into the Barbaricum. Finally, economic factors demanded defended borders. Emperors might not be schooled in the finer points of free-market economics but they fully grasped the state's need to raise taxes and the difficulty of raising taxes from lands devastated by barbarian raids.

The problem is that perimeter defence requires large troop numbers. In any one local zone, forces must be sufficiently large to (i) be strung out along the frontier as a trip wire and (ii) be able to concentrate quickly enough to hold off an average-sized raiding force. Exactly how many troops are required in each place depends on various factors such as the scale of the threat and the mobilisation speed of the defenders. One reason the Empire favoured river boundaries is that soldiers could easily be shuttled up and down by boats. In other locations, the army laid roads along the border for the same purpose.

With perimeter defence, the total size of the defending army will be considerably larger than the sum total of the mobile raiding forces that thrust into Imperial territory at a time and place of their choosing.

In short, Roman warfare switched from a profit-making enterprise to an expensive financial liability.

History of the Crisis

The narrative history of the third century crisis is well known so will only be briefly summarised here. The assassination of Severus Alexander by his own soldiers in 235 is generally considered to mark the precipitation of the crisis. The assassins promptly made the commander of the Legio IV Italica, one Maximinus, the first 'barrack-room' emperor in his place. The point about Maximinus is that he was not related to the Severans or any Imperial family, not a Roman aristocrat, had zero experience of political administration, and was not even from one of the great Mediterranean cities but from Thracia (or thereabouts). His sole claim to the throne was the support of the army. From Maximinus on, there was no pretence of civilian involvement in the choice of emperor; anyone with the backing of enough troops could seize power.

Maximinus lasted barely three years, assassinated by his own soldiers when he failed to ensure their food supply. The aristocracy attempted to put their own candidates on the throne, starting with Gordian I & II in North Africa. They fell when III Augusta massacred their amateur militia drawn from hastily armed clients and field workers. The senate responded by raising two of their own colleagues, Pupienus and Balbinus, to the purple. The Praetorian Guard murdered them within months. Finally, Gordian III succeeded, serving as a senatorial front-man until killed in battle with the Sassanids.

During the half century of the crisis, historians recognise around twenty official emperors, not including a plethora of failed usurpers. Continuous civil war drained the energy of the army. Germanic tribes pierced the Rhine and Danube frontiers in raids and migrations while Sassanid Persia attacked the eastern provinces.

From AD 249 to at least 262, the Plague of Cyprian ravaged the Empire. A contemporary witness, Pontius of Carthage wrote,

> 'There broke out a dreadful plague, and excessive destruction of a hateful disease invaded every house in succession of the trembling populace, carrying off day by day with abrupt attack numberless people... All were shuddering, fleeing, shunning the contagion, impiously exposing their own friends, as if with the exclusion of the person who was sure to die of the plague, one could exclude death itself also. There lay about the meanwhile, over the whole city, no longer bodies, but the carcasses of many.'

The agent is impossible now to determine with any certainty, but the symptoms (vomiting, diarrhoea, bleeding, weakness, throat ulcers and loss of hearing/sight) fit a contagious virus such as a filovirus like Ebola, measles, smallpox or just influenza. The disease rocketed through communities with astonishing rapidity peaking in winter in a series of pulses rather like modern influenza only with far more serious effects.

The plague entered the Empire via Egypt; archaeologists discovered a lime-treated mass grave of incinerated bodies from the third century near Thebes. It is recorded in Alexandria in 249, reaching Rome in 251 no doubt via shipping. A devastating casualty rate afflicted the Empire. Five thousand deaths a day are claimed by an Athenian writer and the Bishop of Alexandria claimed that the disaster depopulated the city by 50 per cent or more (Harper, 2017).

In 251 Emperor Decius fell when King Cniva of the Goths smashed three legions and auxiliaries at Abritus near the Danube frontier. In 252, Sharpur I of Persia invaded Syria and Gothic tribes raided deep into Anatolia and the Balkans. In 256 Alemanni and Franks devastated northern Gaul, and in 260 Sharpur defeated and captured Emperor Valerian at the Battle of Edessa. Barbarian raiders reputedly reached as far south as Rome itself.

In 260 a Roman army commanded by Postumus and Genialis intercepted and destroyed a large Germanic raiding force of Juthungians laden down with loot from Italy. Nominally, the Emperor Gallienus' son Soloninus ruled the west – as advised by his praetorian prefect, Silvanus.

Postumus distributed the recaptured loot as booty to his troops – presumably the original Roman owners could go whistle. Prodded by Silvanus, Soloninus demanded said loot be turned over to Imperial authorities, i.e. himself. Postumus 'reluctantly' allowed his troops to raise him to the purple, attacked Cologne and killed Soloninus and Silvanus. Gaul, and all the provinces west of the Rhine, Britannia and Hispania, backed Postumus, breaking with Rome and creating the Gallic Empire.

The Gallic Empire maintained a Roman identity but Postumus showed no inclination to 'march on Rome'. He moulded an independent western 'Roman Empire'. After a decade, Postumus fell to assassination and a string of minor generals fought, rebelled and assassinated each other in weary rotation. Spain dropped out early on leaving a core Gallo-British

Empire that was brought to an end when Aurelian defeated the last Gallic Emperor at the Battle of Châlons in 274.

Postumus would not have lasted as long as he did without the tacit support of the powerful landowners of Britain and Gaul. In return he successfully defended the Rhine frontier. To that extent, he perhaps represents a growing dissatisfaction of the wealthy and powerful families of Gaul and Britain with what must have seemed a distant and increasingly incompetent central administration that was obsessed with Persia and defence of the wealthy eastern provinces.

Worth noting is that a victorious Aurelian seemed happy to let bygones be bygones in the western provinces. Little changed and many of the western administration remained in their posts. Aurelian even found the defeated Gallic Emperor Tetricus a post in Italy safely away from temptation. An official 'don't ask, don't tell' policy with regard to who did what in the revolt greatly eased the western provinces back under central control with minimal fuss or dislocation. Nevertheless, this settlement solved none of the political and economic tensions underlying the revolt.

Events in the east are outside the scope of this book. The revolt of the wealthy eastern provinces posed a much greater threat to the Empire. Like in Gaul, the problem started with the fatal Battle of Edessa and the capture of the Emperor Valerian. The eastern armies elevated to the purple two Roman aristocratic half-brothers, Quietus and Macrianus, sons of Fulvius Macrianus who was an equestrian fiscal officer. This was an old-fashioned Roman revolt and Macrianus and Fulvius Macrianus 'marched on Rome'. Unfortunately they never got to try their strength against Emperor Gallienus, as a more plebian usurper, Aureolus, defeated and killed them.

Odaenathus, a Palmyrene aristocrat, declared himself king and executed Quietus. While nominally loyal to Gallienus, the king raised an army and drove back the Persians, reclaiming the eastern provinces. Odaenathus and his heir suffered unfortunate deaths by unknown assassins in 267, but by lucky chance his widow, Queen Zenobia, survived and was on hand to establish a regency around a younger son to whom she had given birth. Zenobia expanded the Palmyrene Empire, capturing Egypt in 270, giving her control of Rome's food supply. This was a step too far and the Emperor Aurelian destroyed the Palmyrene Empire in 272 – celebrating the defeat of a 'foreign' enemy. The Praetorian Guard murdered Aurelian in 275. Six more emperors sat on the throne until the accession of Diocletian in 284, who pushed through reforms, stabilising the Empire and ending the emergency.

Impact on Britannia

During the third century, increasing numbers of small detachments, *cunei*, *numeri*, *vexillationes*, bolstered security forces in Britannia Inferior (the north), that was garrisoned by only one legion, the Sixth (Birley, 2006). Unit names suggest barbarian origins for at least some of them. One of the British governors, probably that of Britannia Superior who commanded two legions, the Second and Twentieth, revolted somewhere around 280. Probus ended the coup by dispatching an assassin called Victorinus in a James Bond-like operation.

This aborted coup raises some interesting issues. One wonders why Britannia Superior enjoyed the protection of twice the number of legions given to Britannia Inferior, given that the only barbarian border lay to the north. What was the threat in the south? Also noteworthy is that just a handful of years after the destruction of the Gallic Empire, the Army of Britain still showed disaffection.

Frere (1984) notes that British cities weathered the crisis more easily than their counterparts in Gaul with little evidence of devastation or economic contraction. One reason is undoubtedly a lack of sizable barbarian warbands crossing the frontier, which is not to say there were no barbarian incursions, but they were raids not invasions or migrations. No evidence exists for climatic deterioration pushing barbarian raids and migrations out of northern Britain. Frere also suggests that an additional explanation is the earthwork defences erected around most British cities by the end of the second century (the latest archaeological date that can be established is 190). Also, British defences typically encompass the whole city or town whereas urban defences in Gaul, where they existed, tended to be small citadels protecting core public buildings.

As mentioned, earthworks are not only cheaper to construct than stone walls but they can be thrown up by unskilled workers such as slaves or conscripted peasantry. That may be relevant if they were put up over a short period and Clodius Albinus is a likely candidate. He first put himself forward as a potential Imperial candidate after a rumour of the murder of Commodius, but news of the Emperor's death turned out to be exaggerated. When a palace coup actually did for Commodius in 193, Albinus threw his hat into the ring. In 196 he crossed the Channel to the Continent with units of the Army of Britain to confront Severus, those being the last two standing. They had a non-aggression pact while Severus crushed Niger, Imperial candidate of the eastern armies. Albinus probably foresaw a showdown on the Continent at some point and constructed the earthworks to protect his base in Britain.

This does not explain why British towns needed protection, nor from whom? One can dismiss the idea that British towns needed defending against a Roman army invading from the Continent. Albinus chose Gaul as the location to confront Severus, presumably because he also had support from Roman army units in the region. Now if Albinus won, the British earthworks were unnecessary, but equally they served no function if Albinus lost because there was nothing left for which to fight. They must have been designed against some potentially dangerous internal threat.

This seems an appropriate point for a small digression to examine possible military and social explanations for the balance of auxiliary units and legions between the two British provinces. Small flexible units might well be more militarily useful to contain the type of raiding, skirmishing and general banditry expected on the northern borders. Legions were best deployed for campaigns involving set piece battles, although it is difficult to conjure circumstances that might provoke such battles in the south. Given the habitual unreliability of the Army of Britain, possibly each legion was set the task of watching the other.

There is a social explanation for the concentration of auxiliaries in the north. As force multipliers, city defences only have value if manned. The aristocratic inhabitants of lowland British cities might have found garrisons of legionaries way more agreeable than auxiliary units. Legionaries at least were Roman citizens so probably had a reasonable grasp of Latin and grasped civilised behaviour, particularly with regard to their betters. The Empire had a habit of press-ganging captured barbarian warriors into the Roman Army as auxiliary units and sending them to far flung parts of the Empire such as Britain where they would have no sympathy for the locals. Birley (2006) gives two examples of captured barbarians parked in Britain: 5,500 Sarmatians by Aurelius in 175 and Burgundians and Vandals captured by Probus in 278. Few urban villa owners can have been too delighted at the prospect of putting up a gang of heavily armed Vandals in the outhouses. If ever there was a case for locking up one's daughters and hiding the family silver...

How much of the Army of Britain Albinus took with him on his enterprise is unknowable, but presumably the expeditionary force would include a decent percentage by quantity. The percentage in terms of combat power would be boosted by Albinus choosing his most reliable troops – veteran soldiers of proven loyalty (to Albinus). Albinus had little incentive to hold troops back in Britain other than to keep his supporters amongst the British aristocracy onside by guaranteeing their personal security, because a tilt at the throne was an all-or-nothing throw of the dice. If Albinus lost, then British security ceased to be his problem and if he won then he would have the resources of the whole Empire at his disposal.

In the event, when the victorious Severus sent a new governor, Virius Lupus, and military legates to take possession of Britain they found chaos (Southern, 2016). Lupus had no option but to pay off the Maeatae and Caledonian tribesmen to restore order. What archaeology cannot tell us is how much damage the new administration did by purging supporters of Albinus and confiscating their property? Very little, if Gaul is any example.

While on the subject of British urban centres, two other changes are noteworthy. During the third century, the buildings within the towns changed. The rows of small shops and workshops indicative of a Mediterranean city with a functioning economy are replaced by large, ostentatious urban villas for the aristocracy. The British Roman city transformed into a state administration centre with dwellings for an aristocratic elite within secure protective walls.

Civilian settlements around the forts south of Hadrian's Wall, *vici* (from which we get modern placename endings such as wick and wich), grew substantially in the third century, possibly partly because soldiers were now allowed to marry, although Sawyer (1993) suggests the large numbers of small units allowed regular patrols that beefed up security in the surrounding countryside. Whatever the explanation, the growth of *vici* indicates substantial military presence in the area. It is worth noting that the military controlled *vici*.

One peculiar change is that in both Silchester and Wroxeter, basilicas were converted for metal-working. Basilicas have been described as the 'quintessential' feature of a Roman city. Grand and palatial, basilicas represented a source of civic pride as well as having functional uses for administration, religion, business, law, and culture such as displays of sculpture: no basilica, no functioning classical city.

The late third century is noteworthy for the conversion of the earthwork defences around urban centres into walled fortifications and the construction of more Saxon Shore forts (Pearson, 2002). The riverside wall, completing the circuit around Londinium, is also dated to the end of the third century: tree-ring evidence shows the wood in the timber piles was felled between 255 and 270 (Hingly, 2018). This structure is suggestive because it suggests a threat from the sea.

Saxon raids on Gaul and Britain started in the mid-third century and the extension of the Saxon Shore system by major building programmes should be seen in that context. The threat may not have been as substantial as suggested by the scale of the response because the Romans did not think in our terms of economic cost effectiveness. The Army in Britain had to be kept occupied and provided free (already paid for) skilled labour. Reece in his Tenth Annual Caerleon Lecture referred to this as 'displacement activity' (Pearson, 2002).

Another interesting conclusion is that Londinium was no longer important as a commercial port – because the new wall inhibited marine activities. The Thames suffered tidal regression through the Roman era but excavation of the 'County Hall Ship' upstream showed the river remained navigable at least until AD 300 (and probably later). Previously dockside facilities had simply been extended out into the river as the need arose so natural processes do not explain the loss of shipping. In any case, it would have been a simple matter to construct a port downstream where goods could be unloaded from ocean-going ships into smaller river boats. A far more persuasive explanation is the decline in trade between Britain and the continent as part of a general collapse of regional trade across the Empire.

The city still acted as an important administrative and cultural centre, as evidenced by the erection of temples, monuments and expensive town houses. Manufacturing still went on but London's population declined as it wound down as a functioning classical city. In this it paralleled urban developments across the island. For example, Faulkner (1996) concludes that St Albans (Verulamium) suffered a sharp decline in both construction and occupation from the early fourth century – 'a defended "post-classical" outpost of the decaying empire rather than a garden city of Romanised local gentry'.

Britain would have been as impacted by reduced agricultural yield due to lower solar activity as the rest of the Empire, but there may have been sufficient excess production to mitigate against the worst effects. The collapse of agriculture in the Fenlands that required maintenance of a drainage system is probably some indication of reduced economic activity (Salway, 1993) but there are few other archaeological signs.

The Gallic Empire must have been under severe economic pressure as it needed to finance considerable numbers of troops to protect its long frontiers with the Barbaricum, yet did not enjoy the sort of tax revenues available to the central Empire let alone the Palmyrene Empire. Possibly the insoluble 'tax revenue versus security' paradox triggered the fall of Postumus once the money ran out.

The recovery of Gaul by the central Empire failed to resolve Gaul's security issue. In 276 a major barbarian incursion is recorded. The invaders sacked fifty or more towns and owners abandoned many villas in the region. Almost simultaneously, Britain enjoyed a construction boom of elite properties (Salway, 1993). The evidence tempts one to speculate about rich landowners fleeing from their holdings in Gaul to properties they owned in far-off isolated Britain – and discovering that the properties demanded urgent upgrading to properly reflect the status of those now dwelling therein. What was adequate for a local manager would hardly suffice for the elite: 'Darling, you should have seen the pokey little dining area, and as for the wall paintings...'

No direct evidence exists concerning the social and economic damage of the Cyprian plague in Britain. We must be wary of assuming that absence of evidence indicates evidence of absence but it is possible that geography and isolation protected the island. The plague started and hit hardest in the east of the Empire while Britain lies in the extreme north-west. Like many viral diseases that infect via the respiratory system, the Cyprian plague was at its most contagious and spread fastest in winter, when few Roman ships attempted a crossing of the Oceanus Britannicus.

On the continent, civilian settlements around military sites were abandoned around the time of the plague, or show social dislocation to the point of losing a monetary economy (Elliott, 2021). Breeze and Hodgson (2020) report a similar phenomenon in Britain, suggesting the plague hit hard in at least the northern military zone, which presumably had strong connections with the army on the Continent. They write, 'Around the 270s, though, several excavations have indicated that these thriving communities came to an abrupt end. At Vindolanda and Housesteads, coin sequences in the extramural settlement stop in this decade, while the excavated areas outside the forts at South Shields, Wallsend, Newcastle, and Burgh-by-Sands along the Wall corridor, at Maryport and Ravenglass on the Cumbrian coast, and at other sites in the hinterland of the Wall have failed to produce evidence for occupation continuing after the third century.'

The large number of coin horde finds is an interesting feature of Roman Britain in the third century but quite why so many hordes were never recovered by their owners is unclear – there can be many mundane reasons for burial, but it is abandonment, the failure to recover wealth, that is noteworthy. The coins might be abandoned as valueless, which is a possibility for fiat money if the coinage changed. It may be relevant that Aurelian changed the coinage in the late third century after an epic battle between the mint workers of Rome and the urban cohorts causing a reputed 7,000 casualties; labour disputes are not a modern innovation. The second reason for an abandoned horde is that the buriers fled the area or died – in other words some sort of social breakdown such as disease, insurrection or military activity.

One final change occurred in the Crisis that was to have a profound long-term impact on Britain was the disappearance of the *Classis Britannica* (Elliott, 2016 and references therein). This fleet, based on both sides of the Channel protected not just the seaways but the ports and coastal areas of Gaul and eastern Britain. Fleet personnel played major roles in the economy of Britain, running the vast industrial complex in the upper Medway Valley, smelting iron and quarrying Kentish ragstone. The relicts of this enterprise – the quarries, blackened circles from the smelting process, and remains of building materials – can still be seen today.

But fleets are expensive compared to armies and effective fleets appear to be a poor investment compared to soldiers. Ironically, the more effective a fleet is at controlling the seas, the less important it seems to those trying to balance budgets, and the damage of scrapping this costly indulgence may not show until long after its dissolution.

The *Classis Britannica* was one of the most important after the two Italian fleets. Mason (2003) estimates a complement of 7,000 men for the fleet in the Principate with annual running costs of 100,000 sesterces (Elliott, 2016).

The last known reference to the fleet is the funerary inscription of ex-trierarchus Saturninus from Arles in southern France 'firmly dated to between AD 244 and 249' (Elliott, 2016). The Medway Valley industrial zone disappears at about the same time as does the fleet base at Dover. Interestingly, Cleere (1977) suggests that the base was 'comprehensively slighted' (destroyed), the implication being that official decommissioning of the fleet took place, not merely withering away by neglect. Whoever was in charge did not want anyone else to use the naval facilities. The *Classis Germania* also disappears from the record around this time.

Ominously, Saxon sea-raiders started to become a problem in the North Sea and Channel. Rome lost control of these waters and never completely recovered it.

A New Type of Insurrection?

Internal insurrection in the Roman world took a number of familiar forms. First were military coups by generals who saw no reason why they should not be emperor, second were mutinies by units of disaffected troops, and finally tribal uprisings. Gaul and Spain suffered a type of uprising in the late third century that seemed to have been regarded as novel by contemporaries: the Bacaudae or Bagaudae. The term may be derived from a Brythonic word meaning 'fighter' or 'warrior'.

So, what or who were Bagaudae? Claudius Mamertinus (the late third century one) called Bagaudae *monstrorum biformium* (double-shaped monsters) because on one hand they were Roman citizens and farmers and on the other they were rogues and rebels. He described the Bagaudae uprising thus:

'simple farmers in military dress; the ploughman imitated the infantryman, the shepherd the cavalryman, the rustic harvester of his own crops the barbarian enemy.'

The implication being that they were a collection of local peasantry getting above themselves, indulging in violent behaviour that right thinking people considered exclusively the prerogative of their betters.

Ammianus Marcellinus describes this phenomenon in the fourth century (AD 369):

> 'Meanwhile the wicked fury of bands of robbers raged through Gaul to the injury of many persons; since they occupied the most frequented roads, and without any hesitation seized upon everything valuable which came in their way.'

Modern writers inevitably explain this phenomenon through the prism of contemporary events. In the nineteenth century, Bagaudae became Gallic (i.e. French) nationalists fighting for the ideals of the French Revolution (Trithemié, 1873). In the twentieth century they were revolutionary peasants and workers fighting a Marxist class war (Thompson, 1982).

Supposedly at least one Bagaudae leader, Amandus, minted coins claiming Roman Imperial titles (Goldsworthy, 2009), but these may be renaissance fakes (Hern, 2013). If they are real, we could deduce that (i) they were not all horny-handed sons of toil and (ii) they saw themselves as Roman, not Gallic nationalists, tribesmen or Marxist class warriors. It is worth noting that Bagaudae insurrections faded away when confronted with regular Roman armies or even Germanic *foederati*, as one might expect from an essentially civilian insurrection.

Moss (2017) in his review of Couper (2016) suggests that the best model to understand the Bagaudae phenomenon is through the insurgency model of Reno (2014) devised to explain failed states in the modern world. This model presupposes certain things: (i) a centralised state – a fair description of the later Roman empire where all authority and power flowed from the Emperor through the military, and (ii) the fragmentation of centralised networks – again this well describes the situation in the third century crisis.

In this situation power coalesces haphazardly around local political/economic entrepreneurs such as local landowners, estate managers, low-ranking military and administrative individuals and organised crime bosses. These local leaders amass power as they gain access to weapons for protection against rivals. Ideology is marginalised in favour of economic goals, often based around control of local resources including land and food.

A physical analogy of this process occurs in crystallisation caused by cooling of saturated solutions – such as a saturated solution of table salt in hot water. As the water cools, it can no longer maintain the same quantity of dissolved salt so the solution becomes supersaturated and unstable. The distribution of salt in the water will be random which means it will randomly be denser in some places than others – random distributions are not 'even'. In these tiny denser zones nucleation occurs – some of the salt forms stable tiny crystals. If the water continues to cool, more and more salt precipitates out of solution around these minute crystals where the solution is at its most supersaturated causing a cascade of crystal growth. For cooling, read loss of central authority in a centralised state and for crystallisation read accretion of power by local leaders.

This model explains why the Bagaudae rebellions are so difficult to pin down to ideologically driven motives, because there are none. The Bagaudae themselves would in this model vary enormously from small bandit gangs to 'entrepreneurs' running an estate or town as a mini kingdom, albeit with a Roman façade. The bandit gangs might consist of dispossessed and disgruntled peasants, runaway slaves, free urban poor or military deserters and veterans. At the other end of the continuum, an 'entrepreneur's' militia might consist of hirelings recruited from all these things leavened by his local clients and maybe some small military unit over which he manages to obtain control – because no one else is giving them orders and a chap has to eat.

Similarly, the trigger that causes an unstable system to catastrophically break down can be anything. The Arab Spring was started by a Libyan fruit seller setting fire to himself. This unfortunate gentleman started the cascade but he did not cause it. To return to our cooling saturated salt solution analogy, the first crystal may start to form around anything: an insignificant speck of dust, a bubble of air or even a vibration.

The model also explains why Bagaudae insurgencies continued to spring up throughout the existence of the later Empire in remote areas such as Gaul, the Alps and Spain. The highly centralised Late Empire with everything structured around the army was highly susceptible to this process as soon as central authority collapsed. Modern first world nations are resistant because power is dispersed and spread through multiple strongly constructed state agencies and private companies with specific constrained social roles. After the June election of 2010, Belgium went 541 days without a central government while a myriad of political parties negotiated. The country failed to collapse or experience violent insurgency. Life carried on as before; indeed, there is doubt whether some Belgians even noticed!

Although the use of the word Bagaudae is limited to the late Empire, outbreaks of social unrest are recorded in the late second century. In 186, Maternus, a deserter, led a Bagaudae-like uprising in Spain and Gaul.

Herodian writes,

> '[Maternus] gathered together a numerous band of rascals, and at first he overran villages and estates, and plundered them; but when he was master of great wealth he collected a more numerous throng of rascals with promises of large gifts and a share of what was taken, so that they no longer had the status of brigands but of enemies. For they now proceeded to attack the largest cities, and forcing open the prisons they set free those who had been confined in them.'

Herodian goes on to suggest that Maternus intended to challenge Commodius for the throne. This seems far-fetched and we may suspect a literary device to illustrate a moral lecture. The Maternus affair was probably far more insignificant in practice but grew in the popular telling as a sort of Robin Hood legend. It may be relevant that an apparently popular Roman board game was called *Ludus Latrunculorum* or Game of Bandits (Burrows, 2017).

The word Bagaudae is never used for Britain, but we have such a paucity of written material to go by, and given the situational and cultural similarities between Gaul and Britain, I suggest that the same problem occurred. The explanation for the function of the extensive earthworks erected by Albinus around towns safely removed from the northern frontier is to be found in protection from Bagaudae or similar. If anything, Britain was more remote and so more susceptible to disruption of centralised authority than any of the other European provinces. The fact that the earthworks were later converted into stone walls suggests that Roman authorities feared further outbreaks even after the immediate crisis.

The violent history of Britain, even Britannia Superior, likely induced apprehension among local Roman elites that trouble could spring out of nowhere and quickly escalate out of hand. Any reduction of security forces within the two British provinces no doubt did nothing to assuage such fears, but maybe visible earthwork defences did?

Conclusions

On the whole, Britain seems to have survived the crisis of the third century rather better than Gaul, its very isolation proving for once to be positively advantageous. The history of the island as the Roman 'wild west' meant that essential centres were already protected, and little convincing archaeological evidence for widespread instability or destruction has been found. Tombstone inscriptions suggest nothing more than normal low levels of 'policing' activity in the border regions (Birley, 2006).

However, there is evidence of the failure to fully integrate Britain into the Empire as a functioning part of classical civilisation, notably the change in function of the earthwork-defended urban centres. Isolation meant that fluctuations in the strength of central control in an authoritarian social system that depended almost entirely on the army as the solitary axis of power gave a high possibility of haphazard outbreaks of insurrection that could rapidly escalate.

An ominous sign for the future was the disappearance of the *Classis Britannica* and the concomitant appearance of Saxon sea-raiders.

Chapter 8

Britain in the Dominate

The Unquiet Island

The narrative history of Britain in the later Empire is a theatre of instability. I will just give a short summary here of what seem to me to be key events or at least those for which some evidence exists.

After the fall of the Gallic Empire, Emperor Diocletian appointed Maximian Caesar and put him in charge of restoring order in the recaptured territories. This involved restoring the Rhine frontiers, putting down Bagaudae insurrections and responding to Saxon and Frankish sea-raiders along the North Sea and Channel coasts. Maximian delegated the latter task to Carausius, reputedly a Menapian Roman army officer. The Menapii were a Belgic people living along the coast from the Scheldt to the Rhine so presumably this meant Carausius had some familiarity with the sea and shipping.

Operating out of Boulogne, Carausius had at his disposal considerable assets from the armies of Britain and Gaul and he built a substantial fleet to serve as a new *Classis Britannica*. This strategy proved effective and Carausius enjoyed considerable support, inevitably arousing paranoic suspicion in Diocletian and Maximian. Popular, competent generals commanding substantial forces kept Emperors awake at night. Carausius responded to threatened recall and execution in the traditional Roman Army way, by declaring himself Emperor of a new 'Gallic Empire' in 297.

The two southern legions, II Augusta and XX Valeria Victrix, and the VI Victrix at York, are depicted on Carausian coins showing he controlled the island. Carausius' coins also celebrate six legions stationed along the Rhine and, astonishingly, the II Parthica based in Italy (Elliott, in press). Elliott suggests that these 'legions' supporting Carausius were probably vexillations (detachments) rather than the whole unit but notes that it does show that the usurper had contacts widely across the officers of the western Roman Army.

Carausius proclaimed his association with the island by minting coins marked *Restitutor Britanniae* (Restorer of Britain) and *Genius Britanniae* (Spirit of Britain). This PR strategy might have suggested itself because the principal Celtic tribe in southeast Britain before Rome was also Belgic, but Carausius' new state was as Roman in culture as any other part of the western Empire. All romantic thoughts of some Celtic or tribal national bid for freedom must be firmly put aside: Carausius had carried out a very Roman military coup.

Carausius enjoyed initial military success against Maximian, who sought to bring the usurper to heel, with a naval engagement. Maximian must have built a new fleet as Carausius had control of the original one. Thus Carausius maintained his grip on the continental coast. Some of the coastal defences in Britain and the continent possibly date from this period. For a while the Empire tolerated Carausius while the western armies laboured elsewhere, shoring up the continental frontiers.

Diocletian introduced the Tetrarchy in 293 giving the Western Empire the undivided attention of its own Augustus, Maximian, and a new Caesar, Constantius Chlorus, who focussed on recovering the lost provinces. Constantius started by capturing Carausias' fortified base and headquarters at Boulogne. This defeat dealt a fatal blow to Carausias' *auctoritas*; his finance officer, Allectus, promptly assassinated the rebel emperor and took his place, seven years after the initial revolt.

Constantine spent three years hoovering up Allectus' remaining continental possessions while constructing new ships for an invasion. He split his fleet into two, commanding one that sailed direct to Kent as a feint to distract Allectus, while the second under Asclepiodotus landed unopposed somewhere in the Solent after slipping past Allectus' navy in thick fog.

Allectus rushed west from his base in Kent (Richborough? Canterbury?) taking only the forces immediately under his control consisting of some Roman troops and Germanic auxiliaries. These are described by Eumenius as 'barbarian mercenaries' although this may be poetic licence tarring the rebels as unRoman – barbarian auxiliaries were hardly a novelty in Roman armies. Roman warlords liked to celebrate victory over 'foreigners' rather than fellow Romans so politics may have driven this emphasis on 'Frankishness'. Asclepiodotus, an experienced professional soldier who according to the *Historia Augusta* served under four emperors, completely outgeneralled Allectus, destroying both the ex 'bean-counter' and his army.

One last twist in the story remains. Some of Constantius' detachment got lost in the fog and sailed up the Thames to London. There they encountered remnants of Allectus' Frankish auxiliaries busily employed in comprehensively sacking the city, presumably in lieu of pay that they had no doubt been promised but would now never receive. The loyalists duly slaughtered the leaderless and disorganised Franks giving Constantius a heaven-sent propaganda opportunity which he duly exploited on gold medallions.

The medallion depicts a grateful Britannia kneeling at the gates of London, arms upraised in supplication to the martial emperor who, spear in hand, rides a battle horse alongside a war galley. Spin-doctoring is not only a modern profession.

Digressing slightly, this example reminds us that the endless civil wars between hopeful emperors were not just a military game of thrones. Considerable damage could be done to civilian infrastructure, not least by the defeated and routed soldiers.

Constantius I found it necessary to campaign in Scotland in 305 after succeeding Maximian as Western Emperor. We know next to nothing about this major military operation. There seems no connection between this campaign and the war against Allectus. A decade-long gap means that the timing is all wrong.

It is difficult to see what advantage Constantius might gain from initiating a war: he had enough problems with internal Roman politics over the succession of his son. He already enjoyed more than enough military kudos from his victories in northern Gaul against the Franks and Alamanni so starting an unnecessary war to win glory is an unlikely explanation. More likely Constantius' invasion of Scotland was a reaction to aggression from the irritatingly rebellious Britunculi. The Emperor took the title of Britannicus Maximus II on successful completion of the campaign so it must have been of some significance.

In the early part of the fourth century, the Dominate system was applied to Britain. The two provinces were split into four (and possibly later five) with separate military and civilian administrations. Provinces were run by governors, *praeses*, who reported to a *vicarius Britanniarum*, a governor of the whole island diocese based in London who was himself subordinate to the prefecture of Gaul.

This reform fragmented authority reducing the chances of any single individual rebelling, but it did nothing to solve the problem of legitimate succession – the successful commander of a large military force always manoeuvred one step away from either execution (to pre-empt any possible rebellion) or the throne (by mounting a successful revolt). Increasingly the military promoted up from the ranks while civilian authorities still recruited from within the urban elite.

The new system promulgated an increase in officialdom. In the Principate a single governor with a single office staff ran Britain: in the Dominate five civilian and two military offices replaced the governor – putting further burdens on a tax revenue already struggling to maintain the army.

The Tetrarchy failed almost immediately when the Alemanni king Chrocus and the army in York quite illegitimately declared Constantine, Constantius' son, to be the western *augustus* (senior emperor) in 306. A new round of civil wars eventually left Constantine I as last man standing after the battle of Milvian Bridge in 312: one of the rare times when a coup that started in Britain actually succeeded.

The death of Constantine I triggered another round of violence with serious consequences for Roman Britain. Constantine I's younger son, Constans, inherited all the western European provinces in 340 – after he disposed of his elder brother. In 343 the Emperor crossed the Channel to Britain in early spring. Emperors needed a compelling reason to visit Britain at the best of times, a great deal might occur on the continent while he was overseas, but for an emperor to make the crossing in person, in winter, outside the sailing season, implies a pressing emergency. A serious risk of shipwreck existed. The Emperor could drown or at best be thrown ashore in some inhospitable place without his normal protection.

Internal insurgency or possibly barbarian incursions probably explain the trip. Emperors did not cross the Channel with a few staff but travelled with at least a reliable army unit or two as bodyguards. A small fleet would have been needed – and all at a time when right-thinking mariners or at least those that wanted to reach old age laid up their ships.

Another round of civil wars started when an army commander called Magnentius executed Constans in a palace coup in 350. Magnentius declared himself Western Emperor but, inevitably, so did two other contenders. Magnentius personally put down one, while the other, who commanded a large part of the western armies, elected to retire and bequeath his units to the Eastern Emperor, Constantine II, in what was clearly a spoiling manoeuvre.

In 351 the armies of the two emperors met in a vicious battle of attrition at Mursa where Magnentius lost on points. Constantius spent the next two years forcing Magnentius back into his home territories in the Prefecture of Gaul. The armies clashed again at Mons Seleucus in south-eastern France resulting in a final victory for Constantius. Salway (1993) makes the point that this was the third defeat in a row for armies of the prefecture of Gaul in civil war, something that can have done little for morale.

Constantius now embarked on a vicious purge of the prefecture. Ammianus Marcellinus records,

'And whether any enemy of the accused man pressed him or not, as if the mere fact that his name had been mentioned was sufficient, everyone who was informed against or in any way called in question, was condemned either to death, or to confiscation of his property, or to confinement in a desert island.'

This was not just a case of removing a handful of Magnentius' senior loyalists, but extirpation of most of the elite of the prefecture, akin to the Great Terror of Stalin. The repression in the diocese of Britain in 353 was especially severe, probably because of its reputation as the seat of usurpers and mutineers (St Jerome).

It is worth quoting a complete section from Ammianus Marcellinus:

'Of this [Magnentius'] court a most conspicuous member was Paul... He, having been sent into Britain to arrest some military officers who had dared to favour the conspiracy of Magnentius, as they could not resist, licentiously exceeded his commands, and like a flood poured with sudden violence upon the fortunes of a great number of people, making his path through manifold slaughter and destruction, loading the bodies of free-born men with chains, and crushing some with fetters, while patching up all kinds of accusations far removed from the truth... Martinus, who at that time governed these provinces as deputy, being greatly concerned for the sufferings inflicted on innocent men, and making frequent entreaties that those who were free from all guilt might be spared, when he found that he could not prevail, threatened to withdraw from the province... Paul, thinking that this conduct of Martinus was a hindrance to his own zeal, being, as he was, a formidable artist in involving matters, from which people gave him the nickname of "the Chain", attacked the deputy himself while still engaged in defending the people whom he was set to govern, and involved him in the dangers which surrounded everyone else, threatening that he would carry him, with his tribunes and many other persons, as a prisoner to the emperor's court. Martinus, alarmed at this threat, and seeing the imminent danger in which his life was, drew his sword and attacked Paul. But because from want of strength in his hand he was unable to give him a mortal wound, he then plunged his drawn sword into his own side.'

Paul was a *notarius*, a senior civilian administrator acting for the Emperor. Martinus was *vicarius* of Britain. So we have a situation where the governor of the whole island desperately attacks the Emperor's man with his sword and when this fails is obliged to commit suicide with same. Martinus clearly identified with the Roman elite of Britain. Anyone in Britain who had cooperated in any way with the government of Magnentius (i.e. potentially every member of the surviving elite in office or simply living around London) could be described as a traitor and punished accordingly.

Roman emperors had nothing like Stalin's NKVD troops or Hitler's SS, so army units must have backed Paul. Maybe troops loyal to Constantius arrived with him. Martinus was a civilian official so it is likely that the people he tried to defend were also civilians, i.e. local magnates and officials.

The fate of an apparently large portion of the elite included execution, exile and impoverishment. Confiscation of property could wipe out whole family branches along with their retainers and clients inflicting devastating long-term consequences for the prefecture's stability and economy. Seized property might be held by the state or sold to surviving members of the British elite or to absentee landlords from across the Empire. Either way, the purge must have had a chilling effect on both the numbers and confidence of the local governing class, especially around London.

The affair of Paul 'The Chain' illustrates the dangers of civil wars not just for army commanders but for all involved – and everyone was involved whether they liked it or not. No one is neutral in a civil war. Civilian elites faced a choice of supporting or opposing a usurper. Backing the wrong horse could ruin an entire dynasty. This was particularly damaging for elite families in isolated colonies like Britain.

Only the suicidal chose to openly oppose a usurper who controlled the local army. On the other hand, being seen to be too cooperative could be equally terminal if the usurper lost – and British usurpers commonly lost. Finally, it should be noted that the winner (or whichever local agent he put in charge) got to decide how cooperative was 'too cooperative'. The scale of judging 'cooperativeness' might depend less on some absolute measurement but more on an estimate of how many estates the Emperor had to confiscate to pay his victorious troops, or just how vindictive he felt.

Every usurpation, every mutiny, every political division, must have winnowed out the Romano-British elites into a smaller and smaller group. This would be particularly corrosive in the south and east around London since that was where decisions were made and fortunes won and lost. Sometimes a nice provincial villa in the far west or north may have been the safest place to be.

As an aside, Julian the Apostate had Paul burnt alive in the early 360s. No doubt few shed a tear.

British agriculture was still in better shape than in most other parts of the prefecture of Gaul, not having been devastated by barbarian raids. The island was perfectly placed to supply the armies of the Rhine because the only effective way to move food in bulk over any distance involved shipping; mule trains and ox carts rapidly consumed the food being carried, mile by mile. From the east coast of Britain ships could reach the North Sea and into the Rhine estuary whereupon supplies could be conveyed upriver by barge.

This may explain why the Emperors of the Dominate were so willing to expend valuable military assets on maintaining their grip on the island, other than the usual reasons of military inertia and the political perils of losing face. But apparently the logistical supply line to the continent failed in the wake of the Magnentius revolt and Paul the Chain's purge.

Back to Marcellinus:

'Julian himself, as it was now a favourable time of the year, assembled his soldiers from all quarters for the expedition, and set out; thinking it above all things desirable, before the war had got warm, to effect his entrance into the cities which had been destroyed some time before, and having recovered them to put them in a state of defence; and also to establish granaries in the place of those which had been burnt, in which to store the corn usually imported from Britain.'

To restart the supply line, Julian first sorted out the political situation in Britain by sending in new officials to clear out a corrupt and incompetent administration (Moorhead & Stuttard, 2012).

Libanius explains,

'After the barbarians took control [of the seas?], they did not let [the grain from Britain] pass. Most of the ships, dragged on land long before, had rotted. A few did sail, but these unloaded their cargo in coastal ports, so it was necessary for the grain to be transported on wagons instead of by river, which was very expensive... [Julian] quickly built more ships than before, and put his mind to how the river could [be used to transport] the wheat.'

Julian in a letter to the Senate of Athens claims to have added 400 new ships to a current fleet of 200 (Moorhead & Stuttard, 2012). Zosimus tells us that the ships were built on the Rhine and claims that eventually the fleet consisted of no less than 800.

So how much food could they have transported? The Blackfriars Romano-Gallic ship was found with a cargo of 26,416 kg of Kentish ragstone for construction in London (Marsden, 1972). Assuming this was a typical Romano-Gallic transport then 800 ships could transport 21,000 tonnes of food by making one crossing each. A generous allocation of food would be about 1.5 kg per soldier per day, so a single crossing by 800 ships could carry enough food to feed Julian's field army of 13,000 for three years. To put it another way, one crossing a year would feed 38,000 troops per year. The Blackfriars boat was a river/littoral transport used for moving stone from the quarries in the Weald down the Medway and up the Thames. Open sea transports could have been bigger.

One begins to see why Britain was regarded as important to the Dominate: no Britain meant no food supply chain which meant no campaign in Gaul.

It is interesting to turn this story on its head and ask not what Britain was doing for Rome but what Rome was doing to Britain by this unexpected food requisition. At the time, Britain was not supplying food in large amounts to Gaul, hence the need to build ships. So where did all this British requisitioned food come from? Was Britain stockpiling food mountains each year just in case the Empire suddenly decided to build a magnificent fleet and come and get it? One imagines not. The food likely came from stocks intended to be consumed in Britain. Perhaps our question should be not 'where did the food come from?' but 'who starved so the Rhine Army could be fed?'

Julian built his fleet in 359 and the year 360 saw another outbreak of violence in Britain. I suspect the events are far from unrelated. Hunger breeds social disruption, banditry and insurrection. The situation was serious enough for Julian to send two regiments of *auxilia palatina* (elite soldiers) and two legions across the Channel in winter. This amounted to about 3,000 troops if they were at paper strength – but as there had been serious campaigning in Germany already, they probably were under-strength as are most armies serving in a combat zone for any length of time.

Marcellinus describes the event:

'The affairs of Britain became troubled, in consequence of the incursions of the savage nations of Picts and Scots, who breaking the peace to which they had agreed, were plundering the districts on their borders, and keeping in constant alarm the provinces exhausted by former disasters... an auxiliary force of light-armed troops, Heruli and Batavi, with two legions from Mœsia, were in the very depth of winter put under the command of this general, with which he marched to Boulogne, and having procured some vessels and embarked his soldiers on them, he sailed with a fair wind, and reached Richborough on the opposite coast, from which place he proceeded to London, that he might there deliberate on the aspect of affairs, and take immediate measures for his campaign.'

We have no further information. Two thousand men (possibly nearer 1,000) is a strange number, too large as a bodyguard for their general, Lupicinus, if he was simply there to take charge and report back to Caesar, but surely too small for a serious battle. Ammianus Marcellinus obliquely suggests that Julian had 13,000 troops at the Battle of Strasbourg, 3,000 of which were cavalry, to give us some idea of the strength of a late western Roman field army.

Cavalry would be more useful for running down Pictish raiders but transporting cavalry across the Channel in winter may have been a risk too far. There is also the puzzle of the rush across the Channel only to stop in London to 'deliberate'. Having overcome the worst and most dangerous winter obstacle, the sea crossing, surely Lupicinus would not be intimidated by a road march through the admittedly inclement English winter weather.

A thousand or so disciplined, elite, loyal, veteran infantry would be perfect for securing valuable southern cities, ports, and agricultural estates against insurrection (deserters, mutineers, Bagaudae etc) while the army in the north got on top of the situation – possibly aided by such southern units that were considered reliable enough to be mobile and combat capable.

In 367, Britain suffered what has gone down in history as the *barbarica conspiratio*, the great barbarian conspiracy. Once again, we rely on Ammianus Marcellinus for a description of events:

'Valentinian having left Amiens, and being on his way to Treves in great haste, received the disastrous intelligence that Britain was reduced by the ravages of the united barbarians to the lowest extremity of distress; that Nectaridus, the count of the sea-coast, had been slain in battle, and the duke Fullofaudes had been taken prisoner by the enemy in an ambuscade.'

Valentinian was the current Emperor. Nectaridus must be the *Comes Litoris Saxonici* commanding the *limitanei* in the south and east while Fullofaudes would be his equivalent in the north – the *Dux Britanniarum* who, if the *Notitia Dignitatum* is to be believed, commanded the greater portion of the Roman Army of Britain.

Valentinian responded by sending a number of senior army officers across the channel who reported on the seriousness of the situation. Theodosius was dispatched in 368/9 with an expeditionary force of two regiments of *auxilia palatinae*, the Batavi and Heruli, and two legions, the Jovian and Victorian – perhaps some 2–3,000 men. They landed at Richborough, which Marcellinus describes as peaceful, and marched up Watling Street to London:

> 'Dividing his army into several detachments, he attacked the predatory and straggling bands of the enemy who were loaded with the weight of their plunder, and having speedily routed them while driving prisoners in chains and cattle before them, he deprived them of their booty.'

Clearly the Roman Army in southern England had conceded possession of countryside near London to small bands of raiders or bandits who were easily dealt with by equally small detachments of loyal troops.

Marcellinus continues:

> 'Convinced by the confession of his prisoners and the information given him by deserters, that so vast a multitude, composed of various nations, all incredibly savage, could only be vanquished by secret stratagems and unexpected attacks... he promised them impunity, he invited deserters and others who were straggling about the country on furlough, to repair to his camp. At this summons numbers came in.'

It appears that many of these 'bandits' were deserters and mutineers from the Roman Army and Theodosius crushed the rebellion partly by offering an amnesty.

> '[Theodosius] requested to have Civilis sent to him, to govern Britain, with the rank of proprefect, a man of quick temper, but just and upright; and he asked at the same time for Dulcitius, a general eminent for his military skill.'

In other words, London, and Britain, lacked a functioning government and new civilian and military commanders had to be appointed.

The final reference in Marcellinus is,

> '[Theodosius] restored cities and fortresses, as we have already mentioned, and established stations and outposts on our frontiers; and he so completely recovered the province which had yielded subjection to the enemy, that through his agency it was again brought under the authority of its legitimate ruler, and from that time forth was called Valentia, by desire of the emperor, as a memorial of his success. The Areans, a class of men instituted in former times, and of whom we have already made some mention in recording the acts of Constans, had now gradually fallen into bad practices, for which he removed them from their stations; in fact they had been undeniably convicted of yielding to the temptation of the great rewards which were given and promised to them, so as to have continually betrayed to the barbarians what was done among us. For their business was to traverse vast districts, and report to our generals the warlike movements of the neighbouring nations.'

The appearance of towers on British city walls probably dates to this period, plus the fortification of a number of small towns. The latter tend to be at strategic points along major routes, eg. at Rochester where Watling Street bridged the Medway on its way from Richborough to London, but not at Maidstone further upriver. The implication is that the sites were chosen for the convenience of the army rather than the protection of local citizens (Hanley, 2000). One gets the impression of army detachments sheltering within fortified bases strung along the road network, as when travelling from city to city they pass through bandit country.

Valentia may have been a newly formed British fifth province or simply a renaming of one of the four provinces to flatter the Emperor. Areans or *areani*, seem to have been scouts or intelligence agents supposed to be keeping an eye on potential threats who instead sold out to the 'barbarians'. They may have operated north of Hadrian's Wall and/or within the diocese. Areani (known only from this paragraph) may be a corruption of Arcani, secret ones (Richmond, 1958). It may be relevant that one of the Vindolanda tablets refers to *miles arcanu*, which could be translated as secret soldiers or secret agents (*miles* can mean state agent in a general as well as a military sense).

So, what are we to make of this? For at least a year, Britain seems to have been in a state of complete anarchy. No barbarian raider could, by themselves, have (i) killed a Roman count (general) (ii) captured (or besieged) the dux (general) of the northern frontier zone, (iii) gained control of the countryside around London and (iv) left the diocese without a functioning civilian government – if there was a functioning army.

This had to have started within the army itself with desertions and mutinies that spread on a north-south axis from Hadrian's Wall to London. This was a Bagaudae-like insurrection, not a military coup. Mutineers rather than barbarian raiding parties would have little difficulty killing one general and 'capturing' another. The mutineers would have inevitably split up into smaller parties to look for food as the supply chain broke down but also to loot portable valuables.

These gangs no doubt recruited disgruntled *colonii* (agricultural workers, tenant farmers), escaped slaves, impoverished urban dwellers and outright bandits. The economic and social dislocation must have been catastrophic. Inevitably barbarian groups on the frontier regions, Ireland, Scotland and the North Sea would be sucked in once word spread of the opportunities for looting and slaving.

Afterwards, Theodosius rebuilt many of the northern forts, partly by using conscripted civilian labour from southern *civitates*. The construction is often rough, indicating hurried or unskilled workmanship. He also erected watchtowers along the northeast coast.

Central Roman control of Britain lasted just fourteen years until 383 when Magnus Maximus, a general in the Army of Britain, mounted a coup. He had served on the island under Theodosius so presumably had a popular following. It may be relevant that many early Welsh kingdoms trace their legitimacy back to Maximus. He took a sizable army into Gaul, defeating the Emperor Gratian. After negotiation Valentinian II recognised Maximus as Western Augustus ruling Britain, Gaul, Spain and North Africa, but in 388 the Eastern Emperor Theodosius I and Valentinian II campaigned against and executed Maximus.

This time Britain remained under legitimate authority until 392, when Valentinian II suffered from an unfortunate hanging after arguing with his Frankish general, Arbogast. There is every reason to conclude

Arbogast tied the noose as he went on to put his own man, Eugenius, on the western throne. Theodosius reunited the Empire for the last time in 394.

The Fourth Century Roman Army in Britain

The Order of Battle of the Roman Army is somewhat tangential to the thrust of this book, but as the army is so central to events it is worth making a few observations. For a full account see Elton (1996) and Southern & Dixon (1996).

The Dominate army evolved from the Principate by elimination of the distinction between legionaries and auxiliaries and the breakup of legions into smaller more flexible units suitable for the military realities of the late Empire. The great set piece battles of the Republic against Carthage and the Hellenistic Empires were over and the primary foreign enemy was now modestly sized raiding parties and migrants. Roman armies mostly only fought set piece battles against other Roman armies, at least until the rise of Sassanid Persia. Coello (1994) makes the interesting observation of the increasing employment of units of the Roman Army for policing civilians in the sense of controlling crowds and riots, this role also favouring a switch to smaller units.

Constantine I introduced further reforms following those of Gallienus, the main thrust of which was to divide units between *limitanei*, peripheral defence troops, and *comitatenses*, the field armies. Units could change status as both were professional soldiers in the fourth century. In theory, *comitatenses* units were completely mobile but in practice they tended to operate in certain theatres and might resist efforts to move them across the Empire. Emperors based *comitatenses* in the interior of the Empire. Luttwak (1976) saw the formation of more centralised field armies as a response to incursion by larger barbarian armies that could penetrate border defences at will. In short, he suggests a deliberate change in the grand strategy of the Empire.

Now it is true that the barbarians formed into bigger political structures in this period largely as a response to association with Rome, but this begs the question of whether Rome ever had a military grand strategy or even understood the concept. Strategy is one of those words that although derived from Greek cannot easily be translated back into a classical language.

The word comes from 'strategos', meaning army general. Howarth (2006) notes that the English word 'strategy' in classical Greek would be something like 'strategike episteme', a general's knowledge – or to put it another way, battle tactics. Frontius called his work on military matters 'strategemata' – tricks of war – i.e. tactics. The modern concept of strategy was first discussed by a French military theorist, Count Guibert, in the late eighteenth century.

There may be a degree of truth in Luttwak's insight, but I suspect the primary explanation for the concentration of elite field units in the interior was simply because that was where an Emperor currently resided and he needed to keep his soldiers close. The most dangerous enemy of any Roman field army was a usurper commanding another Roman field army.

An old proverb usually attributed to the Chinese general Sun Tzu or to Michael Corleone in *The Godfather II* runs along the lines of 'keep your friends close and your enemies closer'. Sound counsel for a Roman emperor, bearing in mind both his friends and enemies were to be found among the soldiers. And if this makes Dominate politics sound like the relationships between capos of the New York crime families then so be it: apparently the director of the 1976 BBC dramatization of Grave's *I, Claudius* advised the actors to base the style of the Imperial family on the Mafia.

If the idea of 'defence in depth', a tripwire of border units with larger mobile units ready to mass and intercept enemy penetrations, sounds suspiciously like NATO's strategy for defending Western Europe – well, Luttwak's book was first published in 1976 at the height of the Cold War. We all interpret the past through the prism of the current. Cold War NATO enjoyed aerial reconnaissance, secure electronic communication, mechanised divisions and the best road network in the world to accurately plot and intercept invaders. Rome still suffered the same old slow communication issues, precluding timely interception of incoming forces by centralised units.

One change from the principate is that around three-quarters of a late Roman soldier's pay was 'in kind' (Collins & Breeze, 2014). Another is that soldiers were recruited locally, especially *limitanei*.

As far as Britain is concerned, the *Notitia Dignitatum* (list of important people) is our less than satisfactory source of information. There are more than a few problems with the document. The British entries may date from anywhere in the fourth century, and bits of the list may have been added at different times. Interpreting the *Notitia* is like trying to get information from a photograph when there is no agreement when it was taken or even if it is one photograph or a compilation of bits of many photos taken at different times. Then there is the problem of non-existent 'ghost commands', useful for defrauding the state or simply boosting someone's status. But for what it is worth, three army commands are listed:

(i) *Comes Britanniarum*: ten units, five *equites* (cavalry), one *equites catafractarii* (armoured cavalry), three *legio comitatenses* (infantry), one *auxilia palatina* (elite infantry). A location is not listed other than in Britain.

  This constitutes the field army, the *comitatenses*. Note that it is a cavalry-heavy force. It would probably expect to go into action in support of *limitanei*. Breeze & Collins suggest that this may have been a late addition to the Roman Army in Britain, created by Theodosius or Stilicho in the 390s.

(ii) *Comes Litoris Saxonici per Britanniam*: ten units, two of which are cavalry, linked to nine Saxon Shore forts from Norfolk to Hampshire.

  – the *limitanei* of the eastern and south-eastern coastline, guarding against sea raiders.

(iii) *Dux Britanniarum*: forty units, of which two are *equitum*, five *alae* and one *equitum catafractariorum*.

  – *limitanei* linked to twenty-five locations along Hadrian's Wall and fourteen other places in northern England, the guardians of the northern frontier zone. Up to 410, finds of coins and ceramic artefacts show a uniformity across the zone, suggesting a unified command and distribution system.

Not unexpectedly, the strongest force is based in the north manning the only land frontier zone. The southern *limitanei* are only about 25 per cent the numbers of the northern troops and are spread out. Saxon sea raids would inevitably be on a small scale because of the limitations of Saxon ships as discussed earlier. An interesting point is that no army units are listed in the west, so who guarded the walled cities and their surrounding villas?

The army normally billeted *comitatenses* within cities so they may have garrisoned the western towns, but surely the field army would be concentrated in the north and east, e.g. London or possibly York, where they were most likely to be needed. Field army units could have been dispersed around the entire diocese in 'penny packets' but this seems to take away the point of forming a separate field army. My 'gut' instinct is that any *comitatenses* in Britain would be concentrated close to London with the senior military officer.

An alternative solution is that the British western communities relied on essentially armed civilian militias (English meaning) for purely local protection. Militarisation of civilian elites is argued for northern Gaul in the fourth century by Van Ossel (1995). Theoretically, Roman civilians were not permitted to be armed, but evidence from northern Gaul indicates increasing ownership of weapons (Hern, 2013).

Another possibility, suggested by Elliott (in personal communication), is that the western *civitas* employed non-Roman mercenaries, the most likely source being Ireland; but Germanic mercenaries, Saxons and Franks are also possible. Ogham is an Irish script found inscribed on monuments in Ireland and west Britain, mainly Pembrokeshire. It derives from the Latin alphabet. Inscriptions in Britain are often bilingual and the script is thought to have been developed in the fourth century in Britain (O'Kelly, 1989). Ogham inscriptions are known from Cornwall, Devon, Scotland and even one from Hampshire.

Rance (2001) reports a detailed examination of the evidence concerning the origin of the mysterious Attacotti. These show up in Ammianus Marcellinus's list of barbarian invaders alongside the Picts, Scotti and Saxons as part of the 'barbarian conspiracy' of 367. Rance argues that the Attacotti are Irish pirates, not unlike the Saxon sea-raiders. In the 360s and 370s the Attacotti attack western Britain and may be the cause of the destruction of West Country villas (Rance, 2001).

From 395, Attacotti are listed as Roman Army units of *auxialia palatina* listed in the *Notitia Dignitatum*. In the *Ad Oceanum* and the *Adverus Jovianum*, St Jerome fulminates against the deviant sexual practices of the Scotti and Attacotti, but he describes the latter as especially savage and barbarous, claiming to have witnessed (ritual?) cannibalism.

Rance (2001) concludes that Attacotti is associated with the Irish word 'aithechthuatha' (subjugated people). The best-known legend of Irish migration into Britain is the Expulsion of the Déisi, a group of aithechthuatha, now dated to later fourth century. The point is that landless Irish groups drifted into western Britain in the mid to late fourth century to become a nuisance and positive danger when they got the chance such as in 367. The Romans settled the problem by incorporating footloose young men into the army and moving them out of the British Isles as was standard Roman practice.

Given the continuous association of Irish in west Britain into the fifth century and beyond it seems entirely possible that Rance (2001) is correct and Irish migrants were settled on the coast to guard against any further incursions from Ireland and hired as mercenaries, thus explaining (i) the mysterious absence of Roman army units in western Britain but (ii) the presence of security as evidenced by unfortified villas surrounding the cities. Alcock (quoted in Rance, 2001) speculated about 'Irish irregulars' guarding Wales.

Finally, it is highly likely that security in Wales devolved onto native kings and their warbands. The association of Welsh kingship lists with Magnus Maximus suggests that such an arrangement may have emerged in the second half of the fourth century.

How big was the Roman Army of Britain in the fourth century? To consider this we need to know what army units were present and their complement. Complement comes down to two separate figures, establishment and actual – the latter always being smaller than the former. I recall a conversation with the writer David Drake, a veteran of the Blackhorse US cavalry regiment in Vietnam. As an elite unit the Blackhorse were overstrength, at least on paper. In practice they were so understrength that tanks sometimes went into battle with only two crew. The sole trooper in the turret functioned as commander, loader and gunner. Blackhorse replacements found compelling reasons to stay behind in the USA, Hawaii or Saigon rather than go 'upcountry' into the combat zone. A constant drip of casualties reduced the regiment's numbers, and not just from combat – military equipment is inherently dangerous.

Then we have the problem of corruption. Keeping 'ghost' soldiers on the payroll is a time-honoured way of topping up the unit commander's pension. Theoretically, the split of civilian officials who accounted for money from the military should have checked this. Unfortunately, civilian officials have pension pots too and a profit-sharing arrangement might be agreed between military and civilians. The further the army unit from central authority the easier it becomes to run ghosts.

Coello (1994) made an exhaustive trawl through the evidence and essentially concluded that the typical actual strength of Late Roman army units is unknowable. Goldsworthy (2003) suggests establishments of *comitatense* legions as around 1,000 to 1,200, auxiliary palatine at 500 to 600, cavalry *vexillationes* at 600, and *scholae* at 500 – with a real strength of two-thirds complement.

In the fourth century, men and units were stripped from *limitanei* in Gaul and Britain to bring *comitatenses* up to strength, so we might expect these units to be weaker. Jones gives estimates for Egyptian *limitanei*, where there is a modicum of evidence, as: legionary vexillations 149–1997 (900?), cohorts 215–525 (350?), *equites* 242, *alae* 354–368 (370) – I have given suggested norms in brackets. I suspect Britain had lower real strengths because of its isolation.

If the *Notitia Dignitatum* is at all indicative of the late Roman Army in Britain and if the estimates for unit force strengths are roughly correct then we can make an estimate for the size of the Roman Army of Britain. Cautious readers will notice an awful lot of 'ifs' piling up and conclude these figures should only be handled wearing asbestos gloves.

The Roman Army in Britain breaks down as – *Comitatenses*: 3,000 cavalry and 2,750 infantry; southern *limitanei*: 400 cavalry and 2,500 infantry; and northern *limitanei*: 2,000 and 9,000 infantry or, in total, 5,400 cavalry and 7,250 infantry. If (that word again) this estimate is more or less correct then the Roman Army in Britain was still a powerful concentration of combat strength, especially in cavalry. But if the *Notitia Dignitatum* is a complete fantasy then so are the figures shown here. Collins & Breeze (2014) estimate 12–20,000 troops in the Roman Army of Britain, working on a model of smaller units than assumed here but more of them, notably *foederati* omitted from the *Notitia Dignitatum*. The military success of the army led out of Britain by Constantine III suggests he had access to a respectable number of mobile military forces.

Rance (2001) suggests that the use of Irish mercenaries in Britain explains not just the lack of troops in the west but also 'throughout

Britain generally in the fourth century'. Salway (1993) also suggested that Britain might have been garrisoned by way of more organised barbarian federate troops than we currently recognise from the 380s. In support of this model, Rance (2001) cites the way quite small Roman expeditionary forces of a couple of thousand men were sufficient to restore order when Britain was in turmoil. If we add in estimates for Irish mercenaries in the west and possibly Saxon mercenaries in the south-east acting as *foederati* then the estimate used here rises from 12,600 troops closer to the 20,000 figure of Collins & Breeze (2014).

Fifth Century Twilight

Honorius was the last recognised Roman Western Emperor whose writ ran in Britain. Honorius reigned but Flavius Stilicho ruled through his control of the Western Roman Army and his connections to the Imperial House. In 400, Claudian wrote a eulogy celebrating the consulship of Stilicho. It includes the usual flattering Roman depiction of the British:

> 'clothed in the skin of some Caledonian beast, her cheeks tattooed, and an azure cloak',

but then goes on to make claims that the warlord had shored up the defences of the island:

> 'You, Stilicho, fortified me... I no longer fear the weapons of the Scots, nor tremble at the Pict, nor along my shore do I look for the approaching Saxon.'

There are also references to the 'sea foaming under hostile oars'.

It is possible that the army campaigned against the Picts in around 368 under Stilicho's direction, but there is no evidence that he was in Britain or indeed that such a campaign actually occurred.

In 401 Alaric, *magister militum per Illyricum* to the eastern Empire and King of the Visigoths to the Western invaded northern Italy. According to Claudian, Stilicho's preparations for battle included withdrawing a 'legion' of soldiers who were 'protectors of the furthest Britons'. That might mean the northern frontier zone, or all Britain might count as 'furthest' to Claudian and detachments might have come from various sources.

The last Roman silver and bronze coins to be distributed in Britain in bulk were from 402 and mostly found in the south-east (Walton & Moorehead, 2016). Very few gold coins have been found dating after 410. Coins were distributed to pay the army and are mostly found at military and urban sites. Numismatic data therefore suggests that Roman troops in Britain ceased to be paid in money much later than 402. This reality is probably key to what happened next.

According to Salway (1993) the semi-legendary attacks on Britain by Irish King Niall of the Nine Hostages should perhaps be placed in 405 and are indicative of rising problems. What was left of the Roman Army of Britain responded in the time-honoured manner by rebelling and raising their own Emperor in 406.

Zosimus writing in the early sixth century in Constantinople states,

'Troops in Britain revolted and promoted Marcus to the imperial throne, rendering obedience to him as the sovereign in those countries. Sometime subsequently, having put him to death for not complying with their inclinations, they set up Gratian, whom they presented with a diadem and a purple robe, and attended him as an emperor. Being disgusted with him likewise, they four months afterwards deposed and murdered him, delivering the empire to Constantine.'

Marcus was a senior military officer of the Roman Army in Britain. This was not a mutiny but a classic usurpation. In essence Marcus' ascension to the purple was a political act probably indicating dissatisfaction with Stilicho's policies that had resulted in troop withdrawals from Britain leading to barbarian raids, especially from Ireland, and the fact that the last coin imports were in 402 meaning the soldiers, pay had dried up.

However, Marcus' coup seems to have disturbed the status quo by setting a dangerous example. He probably became Emperor in the summer of 406 but was assassinated in October of that year (Birley, 2005). His successor, Gratian, was a Romano-British civilian according to Orosius and a member of the urban elite. That would probably mean he was of the curial class responsible for tax collection meaning that he was either bankrupt or extremely rich. This would make sense if, as I think, a primary issue was about pay. Birley (2005) is suspicious that Orosius has been mistranslated and that Gratian was a Romano-British army officer.

The Rhine frontiers collapsed and barbarians flooded into Gaul, traditionally dated to 31 December 406. Barbarian migrations through Gaul flowing past the Channel ports would completely cut Britain off from the Empire ending any hopes of the soldiers collecting back pay. Gratian probably refused to act by invading Gaul, possibly because he was a civilian not a soldier or simply because he thought the policy ill advised. Consensus is that he was Romano-British so perhaps he had plans for a 'Gallic Empire' of Britain independent of Rome.

Whatever, the army was not satisfied and assassinated him in turn in February of 407. Orosius described the new emperor, Constantine III, as a 'common soldier' – in other words a barrack room emperor – implying a mutiny in the ranks rather than a juggling for position among the elite.

406/7 became Britain's Year of the Four Emperors. With each coup, the associates of the deposed administration would have suffered executions and confiscations to pay for the loyalty of the troops to the new government, especially with Constantine's promotion.

The question is, what were the troops 'inclinations'? What did they hope to achieve by raising a usurper? In this case, I suspect their primary interest lay in getting their back pay. They had been left for at least three years with minimal contact with the Empire and, most importantly, without coin imports to pay them.

I suspect that their primary aim was to get their hands on portable wealth and the best way to achieve that was to raise their own emperor who could then get control of the continental taxation system through force. Constantine III led the Roman Army into Gaul following in the hallowed footsteps of other 'British' usurpers such as Albinus, Constantine and Magnus Maximus. To modern eyes, Constantine's military objectives might seem to be to drive out the invaders and restore the frontiers, but his behaviour upon reaching the continent suggests such was not his primary motive.

He took over the administration of Gaul in 406 basing himself at Arles down near the Mediterranean coast where there was a mint. By taking control of the monetary tax cycle at Arles, Constantine could mint silver *siliquae* and gold *solidi* to pay his troops. Some of his *solidi* ended up back in Britain, presumably as pay for his officials and the residue of the army still in Britain.

He shored up the frontier but also closed the Alpine passes with Italy, thus protecting himself from Stilicho. In 408 Constantine's son Constans, with his general Gerontius, took Spain against little opposition. Gerontius is interesting because Zosimus claims he was that rare specimen, a British general. This may indicate the paucity of soldiers suitable to hold rank in Britain at the time and the lack of suitable transfers from the continent.

Honorius, in 409, bowed to reality and recognised Constantine III as a legitimate Emperor of Britain, Gaul and Spain. The year 409 had seen the arrest and execution of Stilicho and 410 the sack of Rome by the Visigoths. Rome was no longer of any strategic importance, but the psychological impact of this act cannot be overstated. Meanwhile Constantine III's empire imploded.

Spain was lost to Germanic migrants and Constantine's attempt to sack Gerontius simply resulted in another coup. Gerontius elevated his own puppet emperor (note that a British general could not be an emperor) and marched on Gaul. At the time, Constantine was marching into Italy – presumably to depose Honorius. Gerontius defeated and killed Constans while Constantine III retreated from Italy. He reached his capital at Arles to be besieged by Gerontius, cutting him off from the taxation system. The Empire of the Army of Britain was over and the soldiers never returned to the island.

Zosimus records what he knew about Britain after Constantine III:

'The barbarians beyond the Rhine made such unbounded incursions over every province, as to reduce not only the Britons, but some of the Celtic nations also to the necessity of revolting from the empire, and living no longer under the Roman laws but as they themselves pleased. The Britons therefore took up arms, and incurred many dangerous enterprises for their own protection, until they had freed their cities from the barbarians who besieged them. In a similar manner, the whole of Armorica, with other provinces of Gaul, delivered themselves by the same means, expelling the Roman magistrates or officers, and erecting a government, such as they pleased, of their own. Thus happened this revolt or defection of Britain and the Celtic nations.'

Exactly what this means is unclear. Obviously Constantine's officials lost power, but what followed? Was this a formal military coup, a mutiny, or some sort of Bagaudae uprising?

A strange after-story is recorded by Zosimus:

> '...Honorius, having sent letters to the cities of Britain, counselling them to be watchful of their own security.'

This is usually referred to as the Rescript of Honorius and dated to around 410. The problem is that this comment is entirely context-free, leading to suspicions that it is a corrupted text, something not unknown in this document. The line appears after a section describing Alaric's advance northwards from Aemilia to Liguria. One suggestion is that instead of Britain the text originally read 'Bruttium', in southern Italy. Woods (2012) suggests that the text should have read Raetia, pointing out that this fits the context much better than Britain, Raetia lying just north of Liguria and so on Alaric's direct line of march. Whatever the truth, this apparent reference to Britain should be treated with a bucket-load of salt.

Pope Celestine I sent Gallic bishops Germanus and Lupus to Britain to combat the Pelagian heresy on the island. The bishops visited the shrine of St Alban (at St Albans) where they miraculously cured a child of a *vir tribuniciae potestatis* – a man with the power of a tribune. Such a man in Roman society could be a military or civilian official. This could mean an official in some sort of 'Roman' society in St Albans such as a militia commander, or it could be a rank once held by the man before, say, his army unit disbanded and so no indication of surviving Roman lifestyles. We will never know for certain. The final episode of Germanus' visit is his supposed victorious leadership in a battle with Picts and Saxons in a 'mountainous' place – clearly not St Albans.

The *Gallic Chronicle* of 452 states that Britain came under Saxon control in AD 441. 'Britain' in this case probably meant the old Saxon Shore since it is doubtful if those in Gaul had much idea of what was happening in the interior.

Conclusions

Britain suffered shock followed by disaster and catastrophe in the fourth century. The fault lines that irretrievably destroyed Roman Britain in the fifth century originate in the constant insurgencies and rebellions of the previous century. On six occasions from 297 to 409 Britain was controlled by usurpers or insurgents, and out of central control for periods lasting from two to seven years. On five occasions, in 304, 305, 343, 360 and 368/9, emperors rushed imperial field units to Britain to put down insurgencies; only one was by a known usurper but all involved societal breakdown and looting.

The Paul the Chain story is likely to be the norm rather than an exception of the purges following a coup. We focus on it because Marcellinus gives us details for his own narrative reasons. A series of liquidations around each insurrection would have destabilised Roman Britain's society, further isolating the people of the island from connection to the Empire. It is not impossible that the dearth of villas around London is the result of purges eliminating local magnates with their property seized and incorporated as Imperial estates or sold to absentee landlords.

The Roman Army presence continued throughout this period although it seems to have lost control more than once, such incidents probably involving desertions and mutinies. The walled, defensible refuges set at key points along the roads suggest that the interior of the island was unsafe even for army detachments. Despite stories of troop withdrawals, Britain never saw the last soldier wave goodbye as he stepped aboard a ship at Richborough. The northern forts remained manned, probably by local recruits, until the garrisons transformed from military units to warbands whose leaders boasted Brythonic titles. *Foederati* remain a shadowy presence but undoubtedly were present, especially in the west, and may have influenced events to come.

Chapter 9

The Archaeology of Collapse

The South and East

London

For this section I have divided Britain into three, the south and east, the north, and the west. This is purely for my convenience and the terms are used loosely. I have focussed on a handful of places that seem to be either fairly typical or, conversely, unique.

London remained the most important administrative centre in fourth-century Britain and chemical analysis suggests that a cosmopolitan population from all over the Empire resided there, which would include Imperial officials and their staffs, military officers, merchants and tradesmen. The *vicarius*, governor of the island, worked from London, as did the diocese treasury officials.

The city was probably the capital of the province of Maxima Caesariensis, requiring a second group of administrative officials in addition to the *vicarius*. At some point an emperor renamed the city 'Augusta' but clearly Londinium remained Londinium to anyone outside officialdom. Pottery and coin evidence suggests that the City of London and Southwark retained populations throughout the fourth century (Hingley, 2018, and references therein).

Coins of the House of Valentinian and Theodosius (AD 364–402) have been found suggesting the tax cycle still functioned at the end of the century with a monetary economy connected to the military and civilian officials.

The city became important in military campaigns in the late fourth century, field armies from the continent using the city as a base or for overwintering. Bastions were added to the east walls, as in other cities in Britain, reusing stone from sculptures, monuments and demolished buildings. Best estimate on dates is that they were constructed in the middle or early second half of the century. A late fourth century second riverside wall has been excavated a few metres north of the original third-century wall.

A structure in the south-east corner may be a protected gateway. Again, repurposed building material was employed. The discovery of a silver ingot of Honorius and *solidi* of Arcadius and Honorius nearby suggests that the Tower of London might be where the treasury was located.

The forum and basilica were demolished and the stone repurposed in the late third or, more probably, early fourth century and the amphitheatre abandoned and robbed of stone. Rather unusually for a city in Britain, a number of public buildings did remain in use to the end of the century and even a new monumental structure erected at Colchester House near the eastern wall (suggested to be a cathedral or military granary). Nevertheless, a decline in the use of stone buildings is noticeable.

The Temple of Mithras was rededicated to Bacchus in the first half of the century. London is recorded as having a bishop but there is scant archaeological evidence of Christianity.

The inhabitants abandoned London, the most important city in Britain, by around AD 410 – just one generation after the new riverside wall was built (Hingley, 2018). The implication is that Britain no longer had a working diocese administration and at least in the south-east not even province officials or administrations.

Richborough

Richborough was one of the oldest Roman centres in Britain, indeed Claudius' army probably landed here in AD 43. The port became an official gateway into the province, a short channel crossing connecting with the southernmost end of Watling Street and then on to London and the north and west.

In AD 80 or a little later (Pearson, 2002) a monumental arch clad in marble straddled the west to east road running through the town to link with Watling Street. The 25-metre-high construction would be the first thing visitors to the island would see as they approached the shore, a triumphant display of Imperial architecture probably built to celebrate Agricola's 'final' pacification of the province. The *Classis Britannica* may well have been initially based here but Richborough became a civilian port once the navy moved to Dover towards the end of the first century.

The military returned to Richborough in the crisis of the third century. Three ditches and an earth rampart protected the Great Arch, converting it into a military signal post or watchtower. The ditches were back-filled in 270 (from coin evidence, Pearson, 2002), levelling the site for construction of the Saxon Shore fort. This would be around the time when Saxon and Frankish raiders infested the Channel after the *Classis Britannica* had been disbanded post 249, but before Carausius built a new fleet and re-established Roman control after 286.

The pattern here as the third century wore on is of a huge Imperial victory monument quickly converted into a military tower then shortly afterwards being demolished so the stone could be recycled into a substantial defensive fort. This was no longer an empire that sought to impress but one focused on the military architecture of survival.

Frere (1991) suggested that the Legio II Augusta garrisoned Richborough in the late third century as part of a general movement of troops from the north and west towards the south-east. Analysis of coins found there generally show a similar pattern to other Roman sites in Britain. The quantity of coins recovered is similar to southern towns but far more than in the northern forts in the fourth century (Pearson, 2002). The implication is that Richborough still retained at least a degree of monetary economy while the northern forts relied more on the *annona militaris* (payment in kind).

We know Richborough was garrisoned in 368, after other forts such as Reculver seem to have been abandoned, because Theodosius landed there. Some 20,000 base-metal coins minted between 395 and 402 were recovered from the site. The presence of a few coins minted by Constantine III suggests that coins circulated on the site until 410 or even a little later (Reece, 1975). Richborough must have been one of the last places in Britain stockpiling base-metal coins either for private or official use.

Fenlands

The Roman Fenlands are noteworthy for two features, engineering works and an absence of large towns and villas, signs that this was an Imperial estate. Of particular interest are the excavations of Potter and Jackson (1996) at Stonea Grange, near the Iron Age multivallate hill fort that was probably the site of the AD 47 battle between Ostorius Scapula and the

Iceni. The Roman settlement dates from around 180–150 BC (Hanley, 2000). Potter & Jackson (1982) discovered a Roman village laid out on a grid with gravelled streets. A gravelled road led to a temple nearby and tidal creeks linked to the site via a canal.

A complex of Hadrianic structures built from imported (to the Fens) stone took pride of place on a gravel island west of the village. This included a large, probably three-storey, tower with all the trappings of an elite building such as mosaics, hypocausts, wall paintings, marble and glazed windows. Nothing like this has been found elsewhere in Britain or Gaul. The nearest equivalent is just north of Rome (Potter & Whitehouse, 1982).

To find such architecture in the Fens is astonishing and indicates not just an official construction but one designed to impress. Potter & Whitehouse (1982) call this 'display architecture', buildings as Imperial statements to awe and impress the benighted natives. The tower must have dominated the flat low fenlands like Ely Cathedral in the Medieval era. That the chosen location is within sight of an Iceni hill fort may not be a matter of chance.

The Fens supported a pastoral economy, raising cattle and especially sheep for their wool. Stonea shows evidence of young animals slaughtered for their meat. Salt production on an industrial scale occurred conveniently nearby so salted joints in barrels could be shipped on the tide down the canals and waterways to the North Sea. From there destinations might include the south-east coast, Gaul, the Rhine and Hadrian's Wall. Stonea looks like a logistics supply centre for the Army (Hanley, 2000).

Around AD 220, the tower and temple were deliberately pulled down. Stone in the Fens was a valuable and rare commodity so would be reused but this fails to explain why this expensively constructed agricultural supply complex became superfluous, assuming it had any purpose other than as an ostentatious display. The Fenlands suffered flooding at this time but archaeology has revealed only limited inundation at Stonea and that may be the result of neglect. Stonea was not entirely abandoned and the early fourth century finds new stone buildings erected but not the magnificent tower. As at Richborough, functionality replaced Imperial ostentation.

Frend (1992) suggests the Fens as the location of the AD 367 military action near London. Saxon boats could have rowed easily inland through the tidal waterways and canals. The Fens offered an ideal hidden base for raiding and when word got back to the continent of the lack of resistance, the initial raiders would be joined by more boatloads arriving more or less independently, adding to the general chaos caused by widespread mutinies in the Army.

The Fens supported a large population in the fourth century but if events transpired as Frend (1992) suggested then they may never have recovered after the 'Great Barbarian Conspiracy'.

The North

Vindolanda

The Roman Army built nine forts at Vindolanda between AD 85 and 213, the last three being in stone, and the site was more or less continually occupied throughout the Roman period (Birley 2014 and references therein). At its height in the 120s the area may have served as a base for up to 4,000 troops and civilians. By the fourth century the fort was home to as few as a couple of hundred of cavalry and infantry. The small *vicus* (town for civilians servicing the military) was abandoned at the end of the third century and not reoccupied.

Extensive remodelling took place to the interior in the first years of the fourth century, barracks being replaced by 'chalets'. Further rebuilding occurred in the decades after 350 suggesting the site was still 'elite'. Vindolanda was refortified sometime after the turn of the century: walls were strengthened and a tower added. Interestingly, structures were erected over some of the old fourth century road network and official buildings, and alterations made to 'official buildings' – the *principia* (headquarters), *horrea* (granaries) and *praetorium* (commanding officer's quarters). The implication is that the inhabitants of the fort now had a local perspective and so neither the road network nor military hierarchical buildings were of much importance.

The *principia* became a residence for someone important rather than an HQ, as witnessed by the addition of dining areas and hypocaust underfloor heating. The implication is that the pyramidal military hierarchy no longer functioned. A church and bath house were built over the old *praetorium*. The western *horreum* became a storeroom on a raised floor (to keep it dry) and the eastern a commercial centre with possibly shops and a market. The implication is that the military food supply logistics to the fort no longer functioned. Iron slag suggests industrial processes still functioned on the site. At this point, Vindolanda looks more like an elite local centre than a military outpost.

An inscribed stone found somewhere near Vindolanda in the nineteenth century and dated to the sixth century has an inscription currently believed to spell 'Brigomaglos lies here'. Brigomaglos is a Brythonic or Gaelic title meaning High Chief. Recent excavations in 2008 found a second inscribed stone within the fort carved onto the foundation step of a commercial building erected in the fourth century but remodelled in the fifth. The inscription reads 'Riacus': the prefix 'Ri' is Brythonic and indicates a king or warlord (rix as in Vercingetorix): the name is known in Britanny as St Riocus.

Implications include (i) there is no discontinuity in the use of the fort into the fourth and fifth centuries, (ii) the architecture started to be remodelled away from a traditional Roman fort in the fourth century when it was still a Roman army base, at least nominally, (iv) granaries became irrelevant at the end of the fourth century presumably because the *annona militaris* ceased when the supply chain failed, (v) in the fifth century the inhabitants included Christians and literates, and (vi) in the fifth century the rulers of the site no longer boasted Roman Army military ranks but Brythonic (or Gaelic) aristocratic titles.

The fort at Birdoswald shows a remarkably similar pattern to Vindolanda (Fleming, 2010). Remodelling of the interior first occurred in the late fourth century. By the fifth century the granaries for the *annona* ceased to be used. One was demolished for its stone. Another was rebuilt into an undivided large room which may have been used for stores or as an assembly hall. Lacking maintenance, the stone buildings slowly collapsed.

In around 450, wooden structures were used in conjunction with such walls as were still standing to make liveable spaces. In a few decades wood replaced stone completely, remaining walls being demolished. One of these wooden structures was an early medieval hall (cf. Beowulf). An elite site still, but the form authority took resembled a tribal chief rather than a Roman commander, although it is possible one was the direct descendant of the other.

Procopius perhaps gives us a glimpse of the process:

'Now other Roman soldiers, also, had been stationed at the frontiers of Gaul to serve as guards. And these soldiers, having no means of returning to Rome... they handed down to their offspring all the customs of their fathers, which were thus preserved... even at the present day they are clearly recognized as belonging to the legions to which they were assigned when they served in ancient times, and they always carry their own standards when they enter battle, and always follow the customs of their fathers. And they preserve the dress of the Romans in every particular.'

There are other possibilities, as depicted in *The Life of Saint Severinus* concerning Noricum:

'So long as the Roman dominion lasted, soldiers were maintained in many towns at the public expense to guard the boundary wall. When this custom ceased, the squadrons of soldiers and the boundary wall were blotted out together. The troop at Batavis, however, held out. Some soldiers of this troop had gone to Italy to fetch the final pay to their comrades, and no one knew that the barbarians had slain them on the way... the bodies of the soldiers mentioned above had been brought to land by the current of the river.'

As to what happened next,

'Hunimund, accompanied by a few barbarians, attacked the town of Batavis,... while almost all the inhabitants were occupied in the harvest, put to death forty men of the town who had remained for a guard.'

Hunimund was a Suebi warlord who formed a short-lived little kingdom until the petty Germanic kingdoms lost the Battle of Bolia in 469 against the Ostrogoths whereupon Hunimund led a mobile warband until he was killed while raiding Pannonia.

One further point is that pollen analysis suggests a reduction in agriculture along Hadrian's Wall after the fourth, the land returning to scrub in the sixth century. The implication is a drop in population and/or change in land use.

The West

Wroxeter

The west is mostly the province of Britannia Prima, although the exact locations of British provincial boundaries are unknown. Seminal excavations at Wroxeter between 1966 and 1990 came to the conclusion that an urban Roman way of life continued until the sixth or even seventh century. Britannia Prima came to be seen as a functioning Roman province until well after the end of the western Empire (White, 2007).

Much is pinned on an interpretation of the restoration and reroofing of the Bath Basilica and its use into the sixth century. If so, this large monumental structure would be unique in northern Europe; all other large structures were abandoned, even on the continent (Lane, 2014).

The idea of a fifth and sixth century functioning 'Roman' urban centre even in a north European rather than a classical way has come under increasing criticism (Lane, 2014, and references therein). The site was badly damaged by trenches dug by early archaeologists and robbers before the later excavations so required a great deal of imaginative restoration that included reconstructive sequences of backfills. This means that the 'stratigraphy' of the site had to be recreated by treating the backfill as upside down layers as if the earth had been removed whole and upended – a debatable assumption.

The absence of Roman artefacts datable beyond the fourth century at the site is particularly revealing. Western sites in use around AD 500 show evidence of fifth to seventh century Mediterranean imports, especially Cornwall & west Devon, and Somerset & Wales. A little has been found at two sites near Wroxeter (New Pieces near Breidden Hillfort and Wenlock Priory, Lane, 2014) but not Wroxeter itself, which is odd if it was a functioning Roman urban site. Similarly, no contemporaneous Anglo-Saxon artefacts have been found, although they turn up at other western locations such as Cadbury that were in use at the time.

White (2007) suggests Britannia Prima had divided into a Brythonic tribal warrior culture to the south-west that used Mediterranean elite imports and a fully Romanised north-eastern Britannia Prima that stuck religiously to 'the old ways', endlessly recycling fourth century artefacts. This sounds far-fetched. Surely somewhere, sometime, some rebellious teenager would have smuggled in the latest fashionable Saxon jewellery or an epicurean of the grape been tempted by Mediterranean vintages?

The parsimonious conclusion is that Wroxeter ceased to be a functioning city at the end of the fourth century – like all the others.

The Wroxeter twilight interpretation fitted the late twentieth century narrative of an Empire that never collapsed but simply changed, something that fitted the academic political climate of the time. There is no convincing evidence of any functioning urban centres from the early fifth to mid-seventh century in Britain – and later in the Celtic west. Note that an elite presence in an old urban setting does not indicate functional urban life; it is the difference between town living and living in what was once a town.

Towns declined through the fourth century. For example, archaeology notably indicates that maintenance on Canterbury's sewers, public baths and streets wound down and that buildings encroached onto the streets, suggesting a vacuum in civic authority (Fleming, 2010). The grave of a family was dug within the walls of Canterbury in the early fifth century. Burying the dead within an occupied city was absolutely forbidden in Roman culture so the implication is that Canterbury had been abandoned.

To modern eyes this might seem simply good hygienic practice, but the Romans had little sense of hygiene. As evidence the conveniently ideal place to locate a latrine within a Roman villa was the kitchen and the practice of communal bathing in warm stagnant pools might have been designed to spread alimentary upsets associated with faecal bacteria and other parasites. The taboo against burial within cities was a matter of religion, or more accurately superstition. The spirits of the dead threatened the living; see the section earlier on the disposal of bodies in running water. Superstitious fear is a far more powerful incentive controlling behaviour than hygiene or official disapproval. The dead must be separated from the living, ergo Canterbury was no longer occupied by the living.

The Canterbury grave is particularly interesting because some care was taken in the burial. The man and woman sat upright in a grass-lined pit. Two dogs had been positioned on the father and the mother held a child – another lay at her feet. Grave goods included valuable Roman silver jewellery and glass as well as mundane items such as keys. One of the children had a bashed-in skull (Fleming, 2010).

After 410 to 420, little convincing evidence exists for occupation of any British city.

Villas

The romantic idea of a functioning Roman lifestyle in Britannia Prima into the fifth and sixth centuries still has a powerful hold. A recent example is the announcement of the finding of a sophisticated fifth century mosaic in excavations at Chedworth Roman Villa (Papworth, 2021), one of the elite fourth century villas around Cirencester. The chain of logic dating the mosaic, which is of itself undatable, is as follows:

The mosaic in question fits a room that had been subdivided off a larger space so the mosaic must have been laid after the subdivision was put in. The archaeologists recovered three objects from the foundation trench of the subdividing partition wall. The first is a piece of late-Roman Shelly Ware pottery, made after AD 360. The second was charcoal radiocarbon-dated to 424–544 with a probability of 95.4 per cent and an animal bone radiocarbon-dated to 337–432 with a probability of 87 per cent.

From this, the mosaic is dated at after AD 424.

An elite industry like mosaics (assuming it is an elite industry and not something anyone could decide to have a crack at) does not exist in a vacuum. If this mosaic was one of a number of similar contemporaneous finds of mosaics or other Roman elite industries in the region then the date suggested could be accepted – but it is not. The Chedworth mosaic stands isolated as a complete outlier, unique in space and time.

A popular aphorism in science is that 'exceptional claims require exceptional proof' as there are always outliers that do not fit a trend for unknown reasons. Do we have exceptional proof in this case? Not really. The pottery is irrelevant and we only have two radiocarbon dates that themselves diverge. With just two datum points there is no particular reason for picking one over the other or assuming that the truth lies in the overlap.

Turning to the relationship between the partition wall and the mosaic, the conclusion that the mosaic was laid after the wall was constructed may be true but other possibilities exist. For example, (i) the room may have been partitioned in some way in the fourth century when the mosaic was laid but before the putative fifth century wall was built or (ii) the mosaic may only have covered part of the floor and the partition wall was built where it is because a nice, unreplaceable, mosaic was already in place and worth preserving (mosaics did not always fill a room, eg the dining area at Lullingstone villa).

British villa size in the fourth century differed only slightly from the previous two, being a little smaller. The number of known villas peaked in the first half of the century, declining precipitously after about 330. Some evidence suggests that the rot started with the smaller estates. The speculation is that richer magnates bought out landowners possessing estates too small to be viable in the worsening economic conditions. This would focus wealth into a smaller and smaller segment of the population, increasing vulnerability and social instability. By 400, the known number of functioning villas had declined to about the same as the latter half of the first century (Millett, 1990, and references therein).

The greatest concentration of mosaics, indicating elite buildings, are found around a line running loosely from Weymouth, Bath, Leicester, to York – the villa zone. They are sparse in the highland zones to the west and north, not unexpectedly, but also in the south-east and east with the exception of the Thames corridor, notably around London and Silchester.

The relationship between the density of villas and the location of urban areas is revealing. There are exceptions, but villas tend to cluster around important urban centres (such as *civitas*, *municipa* and *colonia*) and decline in density less steeply than around smaller centres. This is not an economic relationship as villa density is not particularly correlated with estimated population size but a social relationship. Important administrative centres show the most impressive villa clusters, explaining why second century urban centres are surrounded by fourth century villas (Millet, 1990).

The geographical location of the western villas and their social relationship with important urban administrative centres suggests they were elite country homes but only regional food production centres supplying local urban conurbations including military units. They are in the wrong place to ship food up to Hadrian's Wall or out to the continent. The simplest explanation is that a local elite exercised power in the provincial centres to the west, probably owning villas in both town and country, rather like landed gentry in the nineteenth century.

London, capital of the diocese, is the major exception. Way too few villas surround the city for its size and importance. Imperial civilian and military officials, themselves appointed by other officials coming from various parts of the Empire, held the reins of power in London – not an agreeable location for a local Romano-British nobleman. Never pleasant to be the smaller fish in the pond, especially when one wrong word in one's cups could see one's head detached. Come the inevitable military coup any word could be the wrong one at some point.

Obviously land must have been farmed to supply the city, but that was probably organised by Imperial officials on Imperial estates. Given the distribution of villas, Imperial estates seem to have been the norm rather than the exception around the south-east and east.

The number of pagan temples declines in urban centres in the fourth century but increases in rural areas correlating with the number of functioning villas.

Villages also underwent a boom in the early fourth century. Little correlation exists between villa locations and the many small homesteads, so the relationship (if any) between the two is unknown. The villages are purely agricultural and show little evidence either of social hierarchy or of industry (Millett, 1990). Gilkes (in a personal communication) notes that a villa might be seen as a village clustered around elite buildings; a modern equivalent would be the village of Chilham in Kent with the castle/stately home at one end and the church at the other, the peasantry huddled in between.

Hillforts

South Cadbury hillfort is a large, multivallate, iron age defensive structure that was reputedly 'knocked about a bit' by Vespasian on his 'chevauchée' into the West Country. It was refortified in the latter half of the fifth century and has been part of the Arthur mythology since at least Tudor times. The work is on a grand scale; this was arguably the largest engineering feat in Britain in the fifth century (Anderson, 2013 and references therein).

Whoever ordered South Cadbury built had control of a sizable source of manpower, suggesting an organised, hierarchical society. There are some signs of elite occupation, such as metal-working, glass, imported bowls, and amphorae from the Mediterranean, but equally there is a contemporary cemetery at Hicknoll Slait identified as Anglo-Saxon, although isotopic analysis finds only local people.

The question remains, who refortified the hillfort and why? What was its purpose? South Cadbury hillfort is unique: nothing else like it has been excavated. One romantic suggestion is that the nearby small Roman town at Ilchester flooded in the early part of the century and that the people of Lindinis (Ilchester) just moved lock stock and barrel to the old hillfort. The truth is we do not know who ruled South Cadbury or who lived in it: Saxons, Brythonic tribal or Romano-British.

The fort was abandoned in the late sixth century.

Tintagel is another hillfort site, also unique in its own way, that has a starring role in Arthurian mythology. I have to admit personal interest as I lived for my first eighteen years on one of these North Cornish headlands near Newquay. Tintagel has no signs of Roman occupation other than a few coin discoveries, but two Roman milestones have been found nearby suggesting that a recognised trackway ran past (Thomas, 1993). It is the post-Roman discoveries that make Tintagel interesting.

Current consensus is that the headland was a fortified, elite settlement probably inhabited for brief periods by a local warlord on procession. Well-constructed buildings have been found and a ditch dominated the narrow causeway between the headland and the mainland. Two inscribed stones have been excavated. The second, a piece of slate thought to be a window ledge, has Latin, Greek letters and Christian symbols. Latin words include 'fi li' (son) and 'viri duo' (two men) and names such as 'Tito' (Roman) and 'Budic' (Brythonic).

More imported pottery from the eastern Mediterranean has been found at Tintagel than the rest of the British Isles put together (Thomas, 1993) suggesting that Tintagel was an emporium in the fifth and sixth centuries, a trading port with elite goods coming in and tin shipping out. And this is where problems start. If one wished to construct an emporium in Cornwall, Tintagel is probably the worst possible place to site it.

The smart money would be on a port in one of the superb drowned river valleys of the Cornish south coast that are secure from inclement weather and easy to access. The Fal is navigable inland right into a tin mining area. Today this area is a marine playground with yachting marinas and flat-bottomed river boats – my father cherished such a floating 'gin palace' on the river. The south coast has a hinterland with productive agricultural valleys and copious water supplies. Lush, almost sub-tropical, flora grow in the valleys, such as may still be seen at the 'Lost Gardens of Heligan'.

The Cornish north coast is one of the most dangerous to sailing ships in the British Isles. Prevailing winds and Atlantic rollers trap sailing vessels in bays lined by jagged rocks. There are few good natural harbours, only Hayle and Padstow. Tintagel is not a natural harbour but a rock-lined cove, barely more than a hundred metres wide at its narrowest point between the east side of Tintagel and the Barras Nose headland. Hull-ripping rocks at the low tide mark separate the beach from the channel. Ships/boats are thought to have unloaded at a natural stone ridge known as 'The Iron Gates' which is roughly at sea level on the Tintagel side (Thomas, 1993); the tide would have to be right and the sea calm to unload. There is no safe offshore anchorage where small boats might unload a ship standing off Tintagel Head.

No yachts line modern North Cornish harbours. The locals take tourists for 'trips around the bay' in well-built strong sea boats with covered decks for'ard and powerful diesel engines. Tintagel Head itself is a truly awful place to live with appalling storm conditions. Water supplies are poor, the hinterland is agriculturally impoverished, no navigable rivers give access to the interior and, to put the icing on the cake, there is no local tin. The place has only one big advantage to commend it: it is a perfect defensive position where a few determined men could hold off an army. Whoever controlled this elite site must have had good reason to watch his back! One might seriously doubt whether much of the Cornish hinterland was controlled by anyone living inside Tintagel.

The Plague Of Justinian

The discussion of the peculiarities of the Tintagel elite site makes this an appropriate place for a digression into the role, if any, of the Justinian Plague in the formation of the Anglo-Saxon kingdoms. In 536, reduced solar radiation probably caused by a volcanic eruption seriously impacted agriculture leading to starvation (Abbott *et al*, 2008).

Inevitably disease follows food shortages and the Plague of Justinian swept across the ancient world from 541 to 549 (Stathakopoulos, 2018). The bacterium Yersinia pestis, better known as the Black Death, caused the epidemic. This pathogen probably evolved 20,000 years ago, based on its genetics, and first adapted to humans around 5,000 years ago but did not become virulent for another thousand years (Spyrou, 2018). Recent work on ancient Swedish DNA (Rascovan *et al*, 2019) associates the Neolithic population collapse with the evolution of the bubonic form of the plague as opposed to the insect-vectored infection (the bubonic form is much more dangerous as it spreads quickly through the air directly from human to human rather like an influenza virus).

How badly the Justinian Plague impacted the ancient world is still a matter of debate (Mordechai *et al*, 2019) but the suspicion arises that trade with Byzantium through Tintagel introduced the plague into the Brythonic kingdoms weakening them and so facilitating an Anglo-Saxon takeover – the Germanics being plague-free because they did not trade with Byzantium. Plague has recently been detected in sixth century Britain but, unfortunately for the hypothesis, among four individuals in a Saxon cemetery at Edix Hill near Cambridge (Keller *et al*, 2019). Phylogenetic analysis links the Edix Hill plague variety with samples from France, Germany and Spain, so it probably entered Britain from Gaul via the east and/or south coasts.

In short, any impact from the Justinian Plague will have hit the Anglo-Saxon populations just as badly as Brythonic populations. Given the lack of cities or dense concentrations of people in sixth century Britain, one may in any case reasonably question the severity of any impact.

Loss of Specialisation and Elite Crafts

The Neolithic revolution in agriculture allowed exponential jumps in human populations and the exploitation of marginal environments. Since number and distribution are important properties in avoidance of extinction, agricultural societies replaced hunter-gatherer lifestyles. Farming may have been more labour-intensive than hunter-gathering but, nevertheless, free-time multiplied by the jump in both numbers and population density released sufficient labour to build structures like Çatalhöyük.

Archaeology shows no evidence for social hierarchy at Çatalhöyük and it is likely everyone did a bit of everything, but further improvements in agriculture give a surplus than can be dedicated to supporting an aristocratic elite including full-time warriors, 'kings', priests and the specialist craft professions sponsored by the elite such as poet, stonemason, administrator, potter, leather-maker, smith etc.

In the late Roman Empire, the elite and elite-linked professions were bound up in the monetary taxation cycle (as opposed to the *annona*). Briefly, the state paid its agents (mostly the army) in bullion, coins of precious metal valued by weight. These agents then changed the bullion into base metal coins to actually buy things. Base metal coins were fiat-money, units of transaction issued by a state and only of value because the state declares them so to be. Fiat money circulated around the cities and other military sites and was eventually used to buy bullion to pay state taxes.

Places in Britain with a dense enough concentration of state agents therefore had, at least to some degree, a monetary economy. However, in the Dominate a considerable portion of the pay of state agents was in kind rather than money, taxation likewise, and a monetary economy may not have penetrated far beyond elite and military centres – although the copper coins lost and scattered at an unimportant site like Bradley Hill in Somerset suggests otherwise. As Ward-Perkins (2005) points out, whomsoever controlled fifth-century Tintagel may have dealt in elite goods but they did it without coins.

In Britain the whole process came to an abrupt halt soon after 402 when state payments of bullion ceased and base coins were no longer imported. Constantine III on invading Gaul headed to Arles right down near the Mediterranean which was the nearest government centre controlling taxation. He could then pay his field army in Gaul, but that did not help Britain.

Even though the monetary cycle may have been quite a small part of the total economic activity of Britain it was critical to the elite economy upon which the whole society ultimately depended. The cessation of monetary exchange was followed quickly by loss of specialised activities: (i) centralised pottery production ceased, the potter's wheel became a lost art for three centuries, and large parts of Britain became aceramic, (ii) iron production plummeted to the point that nails became a scarce commodity, (iii) stonemasonry disappeared, (iv) administration ceased so taxation of all forms stopped, and, worst of all, (v) the army, the only organisation that underpinned the state, disintegrated.

The end of money triggered a destructive cycle that stripped complexity and 'comfort' (Ward-Perkins, 2005) from Britain. To repeat myself, when a system falls apart it does not float gently down to a new resting level but plunges well below some theoretical resting level in a destructive spiral of cascading events.

Conclusions

The Britannia that emerged from the crisis of the third century showed an empire in retreat. The diocese needed stone and they got it by demolishing Imperial monuments and the gravestones of their ancestors, not by reopening the quarries. Eventually, people acquired pots by tomb-robbing the urns containing their ancestors' ashes (Fleming, 2010).

Town life wound down throughout the second half of the fourth century and the number of functioning villas shrank. The end of monetary taxation triggered catastrophe as it destroyed both administration and security. Urban and villa life disappeared and associated structures were abandoned. Elite, centralised services relying on specialisation ceased leaving the inhabitants with a simplified lifestyle well below that of the preceding Celtic civilisation.

What happened next would have varied from place to place depending on exact circumstances. Simplifying, the forts in the north transformed into walled elite centres, ruled over by kings with Brythonic titles and defended by their warbands. In the West Country, the elite moved into locations with natural defences. The south and east suffered most: the abandonment of London after 410 speaks volumes.

Chapter 10

Tying it all Together into a Narrative

Introduction

We cannot ever know the past for certain because it no longer exists. All we have is the information to be collected from the endless now, and our interpretation of that data. Then we begin to weave stories to link our interpretations into a coherent narrative rather like the sketching games in children's play books where a pencil line is drawn from number to number to reveal an image. The poetic might like to draw an analogy of seeing pictures in clouds.

Asking whether that narrative is 'true' in some absolute sense is pointless. Only priests and politicians claim to know truth. Humble academics know they are 'interpolating'.

All we can hope for are two things: (i) that our narrative is not clearly disproved by some already known inconvenient evidence and (ii) that it is reasonably parsimonious. I use the phrase 'clearly disproved' since it can be a matter of opinion what is disproof unless it is beyond reasonable doubt, to use the legal profession's 'get-out clause'. And only 'reasonably parsimonious' because it might be difficult to discern any degree of difference in parsimony between competing explanations. Parsimony in this sense means the simplest hypothesis that fits the data, the explanation that requires the least number of convoluted sub-hypotheses to explain away anomalies.

In principle, history as a discipline is no worse off than natural science. No modern research scientist believes they are finding absolute truth. Science creates models that explain and hope to predict the behaviour of facets of the natural world. It is not unknown for widely established scientific hypotheses, known as 'core theories', to fail to completely conform with each other.

For example, Newton's laws of motion are satisfactory for modelling the movement of large objects moving slowly such as cars (or apples falling from trees) but increasingly fail when applied to large objects moving at high speeds, such as spacecraft. For that one needs relativity. Now that's not too unfortunate because we can see that Newton's core theory is a limited case of Einstein's. Much more embarrassing is the fact that relativity does not conform with the other important twenty-first century physics core theory of quantum mechanics, describing the behaviour of tiny objects.

And yet, spacecraft are accurately navigated by applying relativity and engineers design predictably functioning computers using quantum principles (despite one's subjective experiences of the wretched devices).

In this chapter I weave my own narrative of the transition from Roman to Anglo-Saxon Britain, to try to square the historical data with the scientific without explaining away either, and to finally try to give a possible answer to the question, 'Why do the English speak English?'

Britain in the Empire

The Roman Empire was a cobbled-together, ramshackle construction created by a political genius, Augustus, out of the failed state of the Roman Republic. The Emperor functioned as chief executive and head of state but had no constitutional position so there was no legitimate way of removing a failing emperor, except by assassination, or of appointing a replacement upon his death.

All sorts of ideas were tried, including the hereditary principle, adoption to appoint a successor, and acclamation by the senate. Few emperors died of old age so they inevitably became increasingly paranoiac during their rules, seeing plots everywhere. Fear of being accused of plotting often forced important people into rebellion purely as a self-protection measure; one might as well be hung for a sheep as a lamb. A perpetual cull of the ruling families ensued.

Economically, the Empire was founded on exploitative conquest. Military invasions of civilised states enriched all involved (except the citizens of the invaded state of course, but their opinion did not count) and acted as a net input of wealth. Initially Rome saw no reason why this should not continue indefinitely, but eventually reality kicked in as it tends to do. The Empire became bounded by geography to the south and west (the Sahara and the Atlantic), no states worth conquering to the north

(Scotland and Germany) and a state too powerful to be conquered in the east (Parthia/Persia). At that point spending on the military became an expensive necessity. The ad hoc, inefficient taxation system hardly helped. Economically, the western economy was a losing proposition from Augustus onwards.

Rome attacked Britain for all the wrong reasons (for Rome). There was no strategic or long-term economic benefit to be gained. Emperor Claudius needed a military triumph for political reasons and everyone else was happy to go along with it because the army and the elite saw short term personal gain in the form of status and loot.

The initial invasion went according to plan and lowland Britain was conquered after a single set piece battle on the Medway, with everything falling into place within a year by mopping-up operations. The Empire probably intended to use the Fosse Way as a stop line since there was neither glory nor much in the way of loot to be found marching around the barbarous uplands.

Unfortunately the Britunculi had not read the script and Rome faced asymmetric warfare organised from across the Fosse Way. This dragged the army into repeated and ever deeper expeditions into the wilderness. The locals in the supposedly pacified zones in the lowlands proved equally treacherous, from the Roman point of view at least, erupting in bloody revolt.

Eventually Rome occupied the whole island at enormous cost of time, treasure and blood. Holding down the far north proved impossibly expensive, probably for logistical reasons, so the frontier settled more or less along the southern border of modern Scotland – a border that erupted with monotonous regularity. Every generation or two, the army felt obliged to march north on punishment campaigns.

In the first century, the Empire quite determinedly planted classical civilisation into the British lowlands and that meant constructing Mediterranean-style cities. Roman veterans in the *coloniae* had an expectation of civic facilities such as basilica, forum, baths, shops, cafes/takeaways and so on, but Rome also built similar cities for the indigenous elites in the *civitates*. Naturally they kitted these out with the same accoutrements considered necessary for civilised existence.

Hellenistic and Carthaginian cities fitted easily into the Roman Imperial pattern. Greek merchants in Alexandria probably cared little whether their taxes went to a Ptolemy or a Caesar. Here the Empire worked, providing order and security in exchange for loyalty and taxes. Tribal groups in the hinterland of regions bounded by the Mediterranean such as North Africa, Spain and southern Gaul had enjoyed (suffered?) centuries of contact with classical cities so were familiar with Classical civilisation, and could also be slotted in, particularly the local elites.

Britain was different.

Before the conquest, Britain had minimal contact with Mediterranean civilisation to the point that British elite warriors still went to battle in archaic chariots, an obsolete weapon system abandoned a millennium before in the Middle East. The British did not take to cities, which became targets for obstreperous locals, hence the early adoption of defences that surrounded the whole urban area not just a military citadel. London went up in flames twice in its first century of existence, the first time burnt by tribal warriors and the second by unknowns but possibly Army mutineers.

I suspect the Roman cities in Britain failed within a generation or two as classical cities. They evolved into protected enclosures for the elite population, elite crafts, officials, portable Imperial property and the army. By the end of the first century, urban dwellers repurposed public buildings such as basilicas for practical functions like metal-working or demolished them for their stone. One wonders if these public buildings ever served their intended functions.

Britain was an unsafe Roman wild west with a truculent population. The resulting heavy military presence did nothing for relations between 'Romans' and ordinary Britunculi. Modern history provides plenty of examples where occupation by foreign military units has failed to win hearts and minds. Indigenous populations rarely seek the company of groups of heavily-armed foreigners.

The British as a whole did not readily adopt Roman civilisation and the Romans shut British elites out of important Imperial or social positions, probably partly out of snobbery but partly out of fear – who would be mad enough to put a Briton in command of an Imperial army?

Isolation in a sea of unsafe people would not have produced relaxed soldiers. A posting to Britain must have been greeted with even less enthusiasm than to the Rhine or an eastern frontier. I wonder how many middle-ranking officers or officials used their influence to wangle a position in York rather than, say, Athens or Leptis Magna. Not many, I warrant.

Then there is the problem with generals commanding powerful armies stuck out on an isolated island with no immediate superior to keep an eye on them while they brooded on their ill luck. Chasing gangs of bandits and insurrectionists around Britain would never provide fame, glory, loot or advancement. In the long dark hours of the night struggling with yet another insurrection or mutiny, generals must have been tempted to mass the troops, cross the Channel like Caesar crossed the Rubicon, and cast the die.

Even usurpers based primarily in Gaul, like Carausius, had to have the support of the Roman army in Britain to guard their backs. Carausius made great efforts to keep Britain 'onside' even when he operated from Boulogne. The army in Britain and northern Gaul faced similar problems and similar temptations.

Usurpers and mutineers within the army must have added considerably to general unrest and instability, putting further pressure on the province. I suspect that by the end of the third century, or even earlier, Rome ceased attempting to incorporate Britain fully into classical civilisation but treated it as a conquered territory for exploitation of materials, notably metals and agricultural produce.

The fourth century Roman Army in Britain controlled anything with a wall around it, patrolled the roads and secured key strategic territory such as Imperial estates, villa regions and mines. Outside that ran bandit country. This situation was more common in the Roman Empire than one might suppose. Shaw (2004) gives accounts of aristocrats and their bodyguards disappearing while travelling on Italian roads even around Rome. In some ways the roads may have been safer in a frontier province like Britain because the army patrolled them, but on the other hand Italy had far less 'wilderness' where bandits could hide or form large gangs without alerting the authorities.

The modern mind, accustomed as we are to the military use of two-dimensional maps, sees relinquishing control outside urban settings and roads as inherently unstable. Modern armies advance on broad fronts and require control of all the area behind their front line. But the ancient world used point-to-point navigation, called an *itinerarium*, rather than maps. A modern example of point-to-point navigation is the London tube schematic. Many modern Londoners routinely commute between nodes on the tube for years without the slightest grasp of the layout above ground. It is interesting to compare the tube design with the *Tabula Peutingeriana*, the road map of the Empire. Amusingly, modern satnav replicates *itineraria* navigation, possibly meaning the next generation will not have the slightest grasp of where they are in the world.

Controlling important points and connecting roads was probably all that mattered in the Roman world view. It was not so different in medieval Britain (cf Thomas Wykes' account of Henry III's march through the Weald). In this situation, trouble brews in the unpoliced hinterlands, unnoticed by authority until it spills over onto a controlled zone.

The Roman presence in Britain disintegrated politically and militarily in the fourth century. After 350 the damage is archeologically visible. The short-lived villa prosperity abruptly ends with many being abandoned, especially the smaller estates. Essential maintenance ran down in the cities, with streets and sewers no longer repaired. Many unrecovered coin hordes have been found.

The break in the monetary tax cycle in 402 had little immediate effect. For a few years, inertia reigned probably because all concerned assumed the break was temporary, as previously, and that normal service would soon be resumed. By 406 the Army in Britain ran out of patience and a senior officer, Marcus, appointed himself Emperor. This may have been a political protest against Stilicho's policies of stripping the island of troops and so leaving it vulnerable, but equally it may have been simply a strong-man taking control to shore up discipline among disgruntled soldiers.

Gratian, a Romano-Britain usually thought to be an elite urban civilian, assassinated Marcus in the same year in what looks like a palace coup (similar to Alectus?). Possibly Gratian dreamed of setting up an independent Romano-British state, or maybe his reasons were personal. We'll never know.

Barbarians crossed the Rhine en masse on the last day of 406, creating a crisis in Britain that triggered a barrack room mutiny by soldiers. The issue was the cutting of the taxation supply line to Arles and Italy and the loss of the Channel ports caused by barbarian migrations moving down through Gaul. The troops almost certainly wanted to invade Gaul and re-establish contact with the Empire to get their back pay. Unwilling or unable to comply, Gratian paid the price. The new Emperor,

Constantine III, proved an effective professional soldier. He massed an army and ships, crossing the Channel in 407.

At this point it is worth stopping to consider what Constantine actually commanded. The *vicarius* and senior military commander preceding Marcus' coup had authority over the whole province, at least theoretically. As Emperor, Marcus must also have considered himself in control of the whole diocese not least because he would expect to command the loyalty of all military forces on the island (he may have already been the senior army officer before donning the purple). But what did Gratian control?

I suspect Gratian assassinated Marcus in, or close to, London. Gratian must have had the support of at least some army units in the south but I doubt his writ ran much in the west or north. Experience would have taught regional commanders, officials and landowners to bide their time, avoid commitment as far as possible and await events.

How did Constantine raise a field army to invade Gaul? Where did he get the troops? We know of no Roman military units in the west but someone must have manned the town walls and protected the last villas. Be they militia or mercenaries, local magnates presumably paid and controlled these forces for local protection. Such magnates would hardly permit their defenders to march overseas leaving their cities undefended.

Many of the remaining Roman troops were northern *limitanei*. Most of these in the fourth century would have been recruited locally, married locally, raised children locally, and looked after aged parents who also lived locally. These people had deep local roots. How many would be willing to march 300 km south and cross the Channel, leaving their dependants to the mercy of the northern tribes? Gaul must have seemed a long way from Vindolanda.

The key point is that Marcus was probably the last man to claim leadership of the whole island.

I suspect the only troops over which Constantine had effective control was whatever Stilicho left of the field army and the southern *limitanei*. From the perspective of Richborough or London, Gaul was closer than York – the Saxon Shore ran on both sides of the Channel. Constantine may also have recruited Saxon and possibly Irish *foederati* using the portable wealth confiscated from supporters of Honorius, Marcus, and Gratian, plus whatever could be extracted from other members of the elite by a mixture of threats and promises.

Moorhead & Sutton (2012) suggest Constantine's expeditionary force may have numbered as many as 6,000 men. This estimate is based on an estimate of 17,000 to 18,000 left in Britain. This may be optimistic. Desertion was probably commonplace among the unpaid soldiers – deserters are one source of bandits. The southern army strength may have been limited to only 1,000 soldiers scattered around the various garrisons, no field army, and perhaps up to 1,000 recruited *foederati*.

How many ships in the southern ports could Constantine get his hands on to transport the army, especially when word got out through the maritime grapevine of ship requisitions? Logistics alone would impose restrictions. However, in the early fifth century in Gaul even 1,500 to 2,000 trained and armed soldiers and warriors concentrated under one commander would form a powerful army, quite capable of dominating the region.

The point is that Constantine's army was large enough to attract stragglers and even whole Gallic units to his standard. He could then take control of the Arles mint to pay his men but he must have achieved all this by stripping southern Britain of defenders.

A highly successful professional soldier, Constantine proved woefully inept at navigating his way through the political intricacies of high command. In this he reprised the unfortunate fate of Emperor Maximinus Thrax, the first of the barrack room emperors. Constantine's army disintegrated in new rebellions in 409. Immediately, further rebellion took place in Britain against Constantine III's officials.

System Collapse

Once it became clear that Constantine III had failed, the position of his civilian supporters in London must have been impossible. They probably had minimal soldiers under their command, perhaps just a handful to garrison a few key points like London, Richborough and the Imperial farming estates. These units no doubt melted away once it sunk in that no more pay could be expected from the continent.

The effect on the south would be immediate and shocking. No one had the authority or muscle to compel people to stay at their work. The monetary economy on which the elite depended collapsed as base metal coins became valueless without the backing of a Roman state. Specialists couldn't be paid and so drifted off in search of food. Imperial estates collapsed because there was no one to organise tasks and compel people to work. Logistical supply chains broke down so crops rotted in the fields while people went hungry, precipitating further chaos as they scrambled for food. The ripples of system collapse spread out.

You have a dog-eat-dog situation where survival depends on how many heavy-handed friends one can call on at a moment's notice. Society collapses and the Four Horsemen ride out. Small towns, villages and remaining city dwellers suffer badly from banditry and the type of violence that is difficult to find in the archaeological record (cf. the Canterbury burial).

As Lenin memorably put it, 'Every society is three meals away from chaos.'

In the ancient world, the Bronze Age system collapse in Greece and Anatolia provides a graphic example that has been extensively studied. The signs of system collapse include: (i) elite centres and cities abandoned, many burnt, (ii) people (such as the three smiths of Kokkinokremos in Cyprus, Drews, 1993) bury valuables but never return to reclaim them, (iii) elite crafts such as writing disappear, (iv) the socio-economy simplifies and long-distance trade collapses, (iv) depopulation and mass migration happen and (vi) whole civilisations vanish (cf. the Hittite Empire), their successors even speaking a different language.

System collapse is not a cause but a result – a result of processes putting civilisation into an irrecoverable destructive spiral. This can happen quickly after a trigger that may not in itself be the primary cause of collapse. Any system is most vulnerable if it has a limited number of core processes. Using both belt and braces to hold up one's trousers is much safer. If the probability of either the belt or the braces failing is 10 per cent then the probability of them both failing simultaneously is not an intuitive 5 per cent but actually 1 per cent. Add another set of braces and the probability of all three failing together is 0.1 per cent. However, make the error of attaching one's braces to one's belt and the probability of debagging remains at 10 per cent no matter how many pairs of braces are employed. The DC10 airliner had three sets of flight control hydraulics so the probability of all three failing simultaneously was infinitesimal. Unfortunately, all three passed close together right under the tail engine. In 1989, United Airlines Flight 232 suffered a tail engine failure that knocked out all three-flight control hydraulics simultaneously. The aircraft's metaphorical braces had been attached to its belt.

An evolving system that comes under pressure often survives by specialising to increase efficiency. Over evolutionary time, species specialise more and more into narrower and narrower niches which they can exploit more efficiently than any competitor. This has the effect of reducing general ecosystem biodiversity.

Then comes the inevitable ecological downturn simplifying the system and a number of species find their narrow niche has disappeared. A big enough crash causes a great extinction – an ecological system failure. A few generalist species survive to radiate in their turn into a plethora of new specialists.

Rome rode out the crisis of the third century by specialising and simplifying. The Roman Army had always been important but in the Western Empire of the Dominate there was almost nothing else. The Western Empire was not so much a state with an army but an army which organised an entire state around itself as a logistics system. The monetary economy and taxation cycle existed to serve the army. Knock this linchpin away and the state could not survive. In a structural sense this was not unlike the late Bronze Age civilisations where everything orbited around a tiny elite who lived in the palaces.

One further similarity. Bronze Age Egypt survived the catastrophe, weakened but still a going concern. Mycenaean Greece and the Hittite Empire on the periphery of the Fertile Crescent collapsed. Similar to Egypt, the classical civilisation of the Eastern Roman Empire survived because it had more varied economic and political lines of authority. The system suffered but retained enough working processes to survive, but the West struggled and Britain on the periphery suffered system collapse.

The Aftermath

Ironically, the military zone in the north was probably the part of Britannia least impacted by collapse. Cities like York that depended on the monetary economy emptied as they no longer served a function; their inhabitants lost access to food when the monetary economy ceased.

The *limitanei* lived on in their forts growing their own food and/or receiving a local *annona* from the surrounding villages in exchange for security (not least from the soldiers themselves). The lack of coin finds suggests the economy on Hadrian's Wall was not money-based by 400.

Even fifty well-armed, trained and disciplined Roman soldiers would dominate a local area. Synesius of Cyrene in the fifth century records one unit of *limitanei* only ninety strong that he considered the most effective combat unit in the province of Cyrene during a time of intensive raiding. *Limitanei* forts transformed into walled towns and the commander and soldiers changed into an elite Brythonic king with a warband until eventually they were absorbed into new political structures.

Something rather different happened in the west. I speculate that the concentration of wealth into a smaller number of large estates after AD 350 mirrors concentration of political power into a handful of families. Magnates secured themselves by means of personal *comitatenses* of *bucellarii* – private armies of mercenaries loyal to the magnate not to the state or civitates. These warbands need not have been all that large to be effective; fifty men would suffice. Traditional Roman politics suggests that in each local area such as a *civitas* vicious infighting among the elite would further cull them into a handful of families or even just one.

Bucellarii duties would include keeping the magnate's tenant farmers and clients under control, dealing with any raiders that made it inland to the villa zone, keeping an eye on unduly ambitious relatives, and protecting the magnate's property from Roman competitors. Laycock (2012) likens the collapse of Britain in the fifth century to that of Yugoslavia in much more recent times: both were failed states. Gilkes (in a personal communication) observed a similar phenomenon in Albania. Higher authority existed only as a concept, real power and decision making occurred at the local level.

Laycock is undoubtedly correct: Britannia was a failed state. He also notes that military artefacts tend to be found around the edge of the *civitas*, suggesting conflict between them which he ascribes to a resurgence of tribal conflict comparable to the ethnic conflict in Yugoslavia. I think that is taking the analogy too far. I do not see tribal chiefs commanding warriors but Roman magnates commanding armies consisting of a core of professional *bucellarii*, supplemented by armed retainers as necessary. But the end result is the same.

Bucellarii were probably drawn from no particular ethnic group. Some would be Roman army veterans or deserters and some tribal Saxon,

British or Irish mercenaries. Their loyalty probably lasted as long as their pay, which would be partly in bullion. But the collapse of the taxation system meant bullion imports of precious metal coins stopped. Of course, magnates would have reserves of bullion in various forms such as coin hordes and the family silver – not necessarily their own family's silver – but at some point it would run out. The traditional Roman response at this point would be to settle the mercenaries on land with local wives as *foederati*.

The problem is that *foederati* may be loyal as long as one has at least the same number of indigenous troops to keep them aligned with their employer's agenda. Otherwise, sooner or later there will be a dispute and it will occur to said *foederati* to question why they are not making the decisions and reaping the rewards. The Hengist and Horsa myth possibly describes such an event. H.G. Wells fans will recall the fate of the squire and his bully boys and the elevation of Bert Smallways to tribal chieftain of Kent in *The War in the Air*. An alternative scenario to *foederati* going rogue is that a Roman magnate's family come to identify increasingly with their Germanic *bucellarii* – undergoing a cultural shift from Roman magnates to Germanic kings. Possibly the Wessex king list with its Brythonic and Saxon king names is indicative of something of the kind.

The endpoint of this process is small local kingdoms with a warrior aristocracy locked in eternal dynastic and inter-kingdom squabbles. Complicated sub-hypotheses to explain away why powerful Romano-British states did not expand east to occupy the empty lands (see below) are unnecessary because such states did not exist. They had neither the resources nor the political will. They were local constructs with local ambitions and preoccupations.

The disaster hit harder in southern England because (i) it had been stripped of soldiers and bullion by Constantine and (ii) it depended much more on the Imperial system of estates than the north or west. Once it became clear the army had gone for good, people could not be forced to work on the Imperial estates. There were fewer magnates with *bucellarii* than in the west (maybe none) because army units had provided security. The estates disintegrated and agricultural output crashed causing widespread hunger, social dislocation, violent struggles to secure remaining food, emigration out of the region, and general depopulation. The Thirty Years War is an example of what can happen, except that southern England in 410 was less organised than central Europe in the seventeenth century. Undoubtedly Germanic raiders took advantage of the situation exacerbating the chaos.

Isolated villages in peripheral areas probably had a reasonable chance of survival because subsistence farming was the one thing they knew how to do, but these villages had relied heavily on centralised Imperial specialisation for craft products such as iron goods or pottery. After the crash, the villages were beached flotsam with minimal scope for development, unable to replace such mundane but vital items as nails. They were the 'fag end' of a failed state, completely isolated by the sea from the remains of the Empire: how many ships were left in Britain after Constantine's expedition and Saxon raiding? The Roman-British in the south and east hung on like the residents of a metaphorical cul de sac after the road outside linking them to the centre collapsed.

Molecular Biology Date for the Admixture of Saxons and Indigenous British

Once the raiding phase had finished because there was nothing left to loot, Anglo-Saxons arrived as migrants into effectively empty lands in the south and east. This was a completely different process to the Franks taking over Gaul. The Franks took over what was still largely a going concern, especially in the south. They had a long history of interactions with the Empire, including from within it, and for many Roman landowners dealing with a Frankish warlord may not have been so different from negotiations with the late Roman Army who may have in any case been largely Germanic from the general downwards. Marcellinus tells a story of how one Roman town in the fourth century refused to let Julian's Roman Army within because they did not recognise the troops as 'Roman'.

A quite different situation transpired in Britain with migrants from beyond the Empire who had enjoyed minimal contact with Rome moving in to empty space. There was no particular reason for much interaction to take place between remaining British villagers and the newcomers. Neither was a hierarchical society with kings and warriors and neither coveted anything the other had. They had no shared language such as Vulgar Latin, no shared religion, indeed no shared culture at all, so although the Saxon migrations started as early as 420 (Fleming, 2010) the two cultures failed to intermarry, hence separated gene pools.

And that's why the historical and molecular evidence does not align in time.

The Saxon migrants prospered and developed culturally because they (i) brought a simple but fully functioning culture with them and (ii) had the ability to import such resources as they needed from the continent (people, goods, skills etc). By 600 the Anglo-Saxons had hierarchical societies with kings and aristocratic warrior elites (cf. the Sutton Hoo ship burial). This was also the period when Anglo-Saxon states were large enough to 'rub up' against each other. Serious warfare erupts between kings of Wessex, Mercia, the South Saxons, the 'Welsh', and so on.

By the middle of the seventh century, Welsh Gwynedd and Saxon Mercia were allied against Saxon Northumberland. Note the similar military and organisational structures of the three kingdoms and that it was not a simple Celt versus Saxon conflict.

At this point I will digress slightly, and point out that the battle (siege?) of Badon Hill does not fit this narrative, being way too early (AD 500?). However, the information about this event comes from the cleric Gildas' *De Excidio et Conquestu Britanniae*, and Gildas was not writing history. His work is classically 'Classical' in that it has two functions: (i) to convey a moral, in this case a religious message and (ii) to create a work of art demonstrating the education of the author. Halsall (2013b) subjects the work to a thorough and insightful examination. I doubt Badon Hill, if it occurred at all, was any more than a skirmish between warbands: it could describe a confrontation between a magnate's *bucellarii* and another's *foederati*, for example.

The Anglo-Saxon chronicles were not compiled until the end of the ninth century, so reports of battles in the fifth and sixth centuries must be regarded as imaginary. The Welsh kings claimed descent and hence authority and legitimacy from Roman generals and emperors, and the Franks similarly. The new line of Anglo-Saxon kings must have been desperate to boast elite ancestry to match. Tales of migrant ancestors from a German marsh arriving in a rowing boat just wouldn't cut it in royal society. The Saxons therefore created a fanciful history of mighty warrior warlords invading, conquering and laying waste to all and sundry. Fleming (2010) refers to this as inventing a 'brand new past', one necessary to show the legitimacy of the new Saxon kingdoms and their ruling families.

However, the rise of Anglo-Saxon hierarchical societies with kings and warrior elites from around AD 600 cannot be made to fit the molecular predictions from GLOBETROTTER, which suggested that substantial admixture did not happen until around AD 800. We have to look for some other explanation for the date mismatch.

Another possibility is perhaps hinted at by Anglo-Saxon place names. Germanic place names dating back to the fifth and sixth centuries tend to be topographic, like previous Brythonic place names (Fleming, 2010; Hough, 2004). This changes from about AD 800 (Fleming, 2010; Gelling & Cole, 2000). Later Germanic names tend to be derived from land ownership, itself connected to the formation of landowning elites in the developing Anglo-Saxon kingdoms. These are names associated with endings like 'ton' (tun: enclosure, homestead), 'ing' (ingas: people of), 'ham' (farm, settlement), 'field' (clearing, open land), 'hay(e)s' (hedge enclosure), 'hope' (enclosed valley) and 'worth(y)' (enclosure). These are commonly referred to as 'habitative' place names.

These endings are usually preceded by the name of an individual or perhaps clan. For example, Gillingham translates as the 'farm' 'of the people' of 'Gylla'; Gylla being a Germanic personal name related to Godrun. These names are no longer descriptive. Gillingham says nothing about topography but a great deal about early medieval claims of land ownership.

The coincidence between the spread of Germanic 'ownership' names and the GLOBETROTTER genetic admixture prediction is tantalising and seductive. Perhaps this is when many remaining Brythonic villages were absorbed into Anglo-Saxon society as low-status agricultural labourers/serfs working for Germanic elites.

There is more evidence in the well-known model of the 'Anglo-Saxon Shift', a term describing the change of settlement patterns between early and late Saxon England (Arnold & Wardle, 1981). Briefly, this model suggests early Anglo-Saxon settlements were located at elevated locations with marginal soils but after around AD 800 settlements with 'ownership' names shift to valleys with richer soils.

The model is disputed (Hamerow, 1991) on the grounds that settlements moved at various times. But a large-scale analysis of data from developer-funded rescue archaeology (Blair, 2014) suggests major changes did take place to Anglo-Saxon settlement patterns in the seventh to eighth centuries. Interestingly, another major change in settlement patterns occurred in the eleventh century after the Norman Conquest giving the 'classic Midland linear village' with houses packed tightly along a street (Blair, 2014). Intensive work at Sedgeford and other locations offer support for a Mid Saxon Shift, or Shuffle, (see Hoggett, 2001, and references within) and it does seem related to acquisition of valuable land for settlement (at least at Sedgeford) – valuable agriculturally but also for other reasons such as a ford.

Saxons probably did not so much displace the British as take over ownership of valuable land. Brythonic speakers become low-status, landless peasants – still working on the land but probably in some sense 'unfree'.

So Why Do We Speak English

In this model, interbreeding and the formation of a single lowland 'English' gene pool came about because of a shift in land usage in the seventh to eighth centuries. The Anglo-Saxons moved into more productive agricultural sites with heavy valley soil. This is linked with the consolidation of hierarchical societies and ownership of land as evidenced by the change in the type of place names.

Many topographical Brythonic or Brythonic-influenced place names will have been deleted by new habitative names in Saxon English, giving a possible solution to Gelling & Cole's (2000) observation that 'the wholesale replacement of British place-names by Old English ones has never been satisfactorily explained'. The driving forces are likely to have been population increase and the increasing sophistication of Anglo-Saxon communities both socially (warrior elites) and technically (eg. the development of Thetford Ware pottery).

The Mid Saxon Shift brought the indigenous and the Anglo-Saxon communities into close association, but while the gene pools may have merged, the British gene pool contributing at least half and probably more to the mix, the cultures did not. Anglo-Saxon culture and ethnicity completely dominated. So how did this happen? I suggest that this was not a merger of anything resembling equals but a takeover and suppression of indigenous peoples by expanding Anglo-Saxon communities.

We have a useful out-group to test this model in the form of Iceland. The Icelandic people are useful 'laboratory rats' for human genome medical research. We have good data on Icelanders' genetics (Helgason *et al*, 2000; Ebenesersdóttir *et al*, 2018). This research shows that 62 per cent of Icelanders' matrilineal ancestry derives from Scotland and Ireland with most of the rest being from Scandinavia, while 75 per cent of their patrilineal ancestry derives from Scandinavia, again with most of the rest being from the Irish and British Isles.

The Icelandic language is a highly conservative synthetic language closely related to Old Norse. Evidence of Gaelic is limited to loan words and to people and place names so has had a minimal impact on modern Icelandic. We therefore have a similar situation to England where a high proportion of the gene pool is derived from indigenous British people but Brythonic had minimal impact on Old English, some place names being a notable exception.

There is one further clue. Ebenesersdóttir *et al* (2018) find that 'settlers of Norse ancestry had greater reproductive success than those of Gaelic ancestry'. To put it another way, there was a higher percentage of Gaels in the Icelandic founder population than in modern Icelanders. Ebenesersdóttir *et al* (2018) point out that we can conclude that 'reproductive success among the earliest Icelanders was stratified by ancestry, as genetic drift alone is unlikely to systematically alter ancestry at thousands of independent loci' (i.e. we are not looking at a few chance mutations).

This leads to the question of why the Norse were 'fitter' than Irish-Scots. We may dismiss better Norse adaptation to a cold climate as anyone who has overwintered in Scotland can testify. However, to quote Ebenesersdóttir *et al* (2018) again, 'Many settlers of Gaelic ancestry came to Iceland as slaves, whose survival and freedom to reproduce is likely to have been constrained.' Human beings are complex social animals and reproductive success depends more on social status than simple ecological 'fitness'.

The gender imbalance (men 75 per cent Norse, women 62 per cent Gaelic) probably is mostly the result of a gender imbalance in imported slaves but may also reflect that status is a stronger parameter for reproductive success in men than women: women can and do 'marry-up'.

The status imbalance also explains the absence of Gaelic from Icelandic. Ensuring one's children were ethnically Norse to give them the best start in life would be a strong motivation in a society divided on ethnic grounds where one ethnicity enjoyed a higher status.

Classical Greek tradition and modern research suggests that western Greek colonies were founded by male Greeks who took local wives (Ziskowski, 2007). Their descendants spoke Greek, and were Greek.

Iceland serves as a model for what happened in the lowlands of Britain between, say, AD 700 and 900. The Saxon immigrants in the south and east had a successful functioning if simple culture whereas the British were a subsistence farming residue from a failed state. Saxon villages coalesced into larger units becoming socially hierarchical and developing kingship and an aristocratic warrior class. We know of Brythonic peoples but of no Brythonic kingdom in the lowlands (note: the western sections of early Wessex may be an exception).

Saxon culture had a higher status than Brythonic British. It may also be relevant that the Germanic word for foreigner (Wealh, plural Wēalas in Old English), although originally used to refer to people of the Western Empire in Britain, became specifically applied to Brythonic people. In modern English the word evolved into Welsh, Cornwall, and the names of individual places like Walton. However, in Britain the word also took on a new meaning such as 'unfree', 'serf', 'slave' or 'servant', indicating a similar status gap between Saxon and Briton as between Norse and Gael in Iceland.

Weregild was compensation paid to the family of a killed person by the family of the killer to end the matter and avoid a blood feud. One of the complaints against Grendel in Beowulf is that he refuses to pay weregild for those he killed.

Ninth Century Mercian Law valued an aristocrat at 1,200 shillings and all churls (non-aristocratic freeman) at 200 shillings. In contrast, the weregild for a Welshman owning at least one hide of land and so paying tribute to the (Anglo-Saxon) king was 120 shillings, if he owned one hide or less and paid no tribute, 80 shillings, and 70 shillings if freeborn but landless. Welshmen in Mercia had lower status than freeborn Anglo-Saxons irrespective of landholdings.

What defined a 'Saxon', as opposed to a 'Welshman' was purely a matter of culture. One was a Saxon if one spoke Old English, dressed as a Saxon, used Saxon artefacts and behaved as a Saxon. Early medieval culture lacked a bureaucracy recording peoples' past family histories: only the elite families had ancestors beyond living memory and even those were invented if one went back more than a few generations.

In Iceland, the descendants of Gaels changed their ethnicity and became Norse, and probably became more Norse than the Norse. People newly achieving a higher status notoriously tend to be more observant of social demarcation lines than those born into the status. In Britain, the descendants of Brythonic speakers became Saxons, whatever their genes.

One might consider it a form of 'Stockholm Syndrome'.

Conclusion

This study set out to answer (i) why Britannia was so comprehensively ruined, (ii) why the molecular data fails to correlate with archaeological data when dating the Saxon migrations and (iii) why the inhabitants ended up speaking a completely new tongue. A narrative that answers these questions while not egregiously contradicting the data is as follows:

Why Britannia was so comprehensively ruined:

1. The grafting of Classical culture onto British culture failed almost immediately because of the island's isolation from Mediterranean civilisation giving a strongly based local culture.
2. Perpetual social insurrection and violence resulted from this failure making Britain an insecure place held down by military force by an isolated army that was itself notorious for mutinies and usurpers.
3. Britain never became a Roman province with a functioning classical civilisation but remained a colony largely exploited for raw materials.
4. The response of the Empire to a climate-driven crisis of the third century was social simplification around a military dictatorship that offered survival in the short term at the cost of long-term stability and resilience to further shocks.
5. Britannia was run by a tiny Roman elite, few of whom were indigenous British, that depended on the military tax cycle for survival.
6. Fourth century continental events caused further destabilisation in Britain, making it more difficult to hold down when the

army was itself under pressure as the Western empire's tax base eroded.

7. The barbarian migrations of 406 into Gaul created a crisis in the army of Britain because they threatened to permanently cut the soldiers off from their pay. This caused three quick coups/mutinies destabilising the diocese, eliminating and impoverishing elite families in the south, and ending any central control over the island.

8. Constantine III stripped the south of military units in an effort to reconnect the Roman Army of Britain with a tax base, and hence soldiers' pay. His failure precipitated a catastrophe in Britain. The monetary economy on which the Roman elite depended ceased so all elite activity and crafts ceased, including the elites' urban lifestyle.

9. The collapse of the elite ruined the south in particular because the region had no security forces left but depended more than the rest of Roman Britain on Imperial activities. No troops meant no security from bandits and raiders and no one to enforce work on the Imperial estates. The result was violence, hunger, emigration and depopulation.

Why the molecular data fails to correlate with archaeological data when dating the Saxon migrations:

10. The remaining Brythonic/Latin populations in the south were clustered into small subsistence farming villages lacking key crafts that had been provided centrally so they failed to develop socially and coalesce into kingdoms.

11. The Saxon migrants moved into empty space bringing a simple but functioning culture with them. The prototype Saxon kingdoms developed while having little contact with the indigenous British.

12. Saxon population pressure in the seventh and eighth centuries, land usage change, and the Mid Saxon Shift led to more intimate interaction between communities and genetic mingling.

Why the inhabitants ended up speaking a completely new tongue:

13. Saxon freemen were socially elite compared to the indigenous villagers that failed to develop kingdoms, i.e. hierarchical societies, so the Brythonic speakers in the Saxon regions became a subservient low-status group who were probably unfree in some sense. Brythonic typological place names disappear, to be replaced by Saxon habitative names indicating land ownership.
14. As in Iceland, the indigenous British of the lowlands changed ethnicity, adopting the higher status Saxon culture.

Final Thoughts

The development of (i) more sensitive extraction of genetic material, and (ii) cheap, high-throughput molecular biology is a potential game changer because it provides enormous amounts of data for sophisticated statistical analysis, something rare in historical research.

However, we have to be mindful of not just the strengths but also the limitations of molecular studies. They tell us about biology, not directly about history. Using molecular analysis we can track the movement of people and genes, put migrations into time sequence, and sometimes give estimates for the lengths of time involved.

What molecular biology does not do is identify ethnicity or culture. Human beings are socially complex and can and do change their behaviour. There is no molecule labelling an Anglo-Saxon, Irishman, Welshman or Scotsman and genetics in itself offers no more guide to language or culture than possession of a particular object.

Genetic markers are used here simply to track the migration of a population from one place to another and give an estimate of the quantity and timing of the admixture of the migrating and indigenous populations. Everything else depends on interpretation of this data in the light of firm historical and archaeological data. Circular reasoning is an ever-present danger. The temptation is to interpret genetic data in the light of historical narratives but then use the biological data to prop up the narrative.

The fall of Roman Britain is an extreme example of the collapse of the Western Empire. The simpler a society's structure and the more it depends on a limited number of key processes, the more fragile it is to external shock. Simplification can be effective in gearing a society to deal with a single threat but renders it unable to adapt as the environment changes.

A modern example is the Soviet Union. Marxist states are simplified because all power and authority flows through the Communist Party, which in practice means the central committee or often the dictator who controls the central committee. The Soviet Communist Party was well organised for nineteenth century 'metal-bashing' industries making it highly successful at churning out tanks in the Second World War, but circumstances alter and everything eventually fails in a changing world. When the Party failed, the Soviet Union collapsed. The same happens with any state where power is 'monopolar', be it theocracy, military dictatorship or fascist.

Modern Western states are considered adaptable and resilient because they enjoy multiple poles of power in different political parties, various state bodies with specific functions, multiple competing private corporations, and so on. Failure in any individual bit is survivable. Oil was supposed to be the Achilles Heel of the West, but it is astonishing how quickly fossil fuels can be replaced by a plethora of other technologies.

A greater weakness may lie in the monetary system. How close the West came to disaster in the crash of 2008 is impossible to quantify. Journalists speculate that we were just days away from the cash machines running out of money – but they did not. Nevertheless, our financial system does look suspiciously like a monopole of power tightly based on a handful of identical global banks who can all fail simultaneously.

Anthropogenic climate change may provide a suitable test of our resilience.

Time Line

(some of these dates are firmer than others)

The Principate

AD 43	Claudian Invasion, Battle of the Medway, Rome declares victory.
AD 44	Vespasian's campaign in western Britain.
AD 47	Iceni revolt in East Anglia.
AD 48	Brigantes revolt in northern England.
AD 49	Colchester founded, Scapula campaigns in Wales.
AD 50	Forum built in London.
AD 52	South Wales declared pacified.
AD 59	Paulinus campaigns in North Wales.
AD 60	Second Iceni revolt, St Albans, Colchester and London destroyed.
AD 61	Battle of Watling Street, Iceni defeated.
AD 71	Campaign in the north, Brigantes defeated.
AD 74	Campaign in Wales.
AD 77	Agricola pacifies West Country and Wales.
AD 78	Agricola campaigns in Northern England.
AD 80	Agricola campaigns in Scotland.
AD 83	Supposed Battle of Mons Graupius signals pacification of Scotland.
AD 100	Roman Army withdraws from Scotland.
AD 119	Violence on the Northern frontier.
AD 122	Hadrian's Wall constructed, 9th Legion disappears from record.
AD 124	London burnt down, *expeditio Britannica* to restore order in the island.
AD 142	Roman Army moves north of Hadrian's Wall and builds Antonine Wall.

AD 158	Retreat back to Hadrian's Wall.
AD 169	Violence on the northern frontier.
AD 182	Mutinies in the Roman Army of Britain, barbarian raids into northern England.
AD 185	British army unit marches to Rome to demand governor of Britain replaced.
AD 187	Mutineers attempt to assassinate Pertinax.
AD 190	Around this time many British towns are fortified.
AD 196	Albinus invades Gaul with British troops in bid for throne, barbarians raid northern frontier.
AD 197	Albinus defeated and killed at Lugdunum.
AD 198	Albinus' supporters in Britain purged, northern frontier restored.
AD 207	Barbarian raids in north, possible mutiny.
AD 209	Severus campaigns in Scotland.
AD 210	New rebellion in Scotland crushed by Severus.
AD 211	Severus dies in York.
AD 215	Land wall erected around London.

Crisis of the Third Century

AD 249	Last record of the *Classis Britannica*, Dover naval base destroyed.
AD 249	Plague of Cyprian commences.
AD 250	Barbarian raids commence from Irish, Picts and Saxons.
AD 255	River wall completes London defences, walls built around British towns and some Saxon Shore forts constructed.
AD 260	Postumus rebels and creates Gallic Empire.
AD 262	Plague of Cyprian disappears.
AD 268	Postumus murdered by his troops.
AD 274	Gallic Empire re-incorporated in Roman Empire.
AD 275	Civilian towns servicing northern military bases abandoned around this time.
AD 276	Northern Gaul devastated, construction boom starts in Britain.
AD 280	Governor of Britannia superior (in London) plots rebellion and is assassinated by Probus.

The Dominate

AD 287   Carausius rebellion.

AD 293   Carausius loses Gaul and is assassinated by Allectus.

AD 296   Allectus defeated by Constantius, London rescued from sacking by refugees from Allectus' army.

AD 306   Constantius dies while campaigning in the north, Constantine mounts coup to become western Emperor.

AD 312   Constantine defeats rivals to secure the throne as sole Emperor.

AD 343   Emperor Constans chances winter crossing of the Channel to deal with emergency in Britain.

AD 350   Magnentius rebels and seizes western throne.

AD 351   Magnentius defeated and killed, Paul the Chain mounts ruthless purge of British elite families.

AD 359   Julian builds a large fleet and requisitions food from Britain to feed the Army of Gaul.

AD 367   Mutinies and desertions in British Army, 'Barbarian conspiracy' of Attacotti, Scotti, Picts and Saxons (probably including Bagaudae) raid at will and devastate the island as far south as London.

AD 368/9   Theodosius arrives with fresh troops and restores order.

AD 383   Magnus Maximus campaigns against Picts and Scotti rebels, is declared Emperor and invades Gaul.

AD 387   Maximus invades Italy forcing out the western Emperor, Valentinian II.

AD 388   Eastern Emperor, Theodosius I, defeats and kills Maximus.

AD 400   Stilicho campaigns in Britain.

AD 402   Bronze and precious metal coins cease to be imported in bulk, troop withdrawals.

AD 405   Irish raids into Britain's west coast, possible date for kidnap of St Patrick.

AD 406   Gallic frontiers collapse.

AD 407   Roman Army of Britain declare Marcus, Gratian and Constantine III Emperor in quick succession, Constantine III takes British Army units to Gaul.

AD 408   Constantine III's forces control Spain, gold coins cease completely to be imported so salaries of soldiers and officials unpaid.

AD 409	Constantine III legitimised by Honorius as Western Emperor, barbarians cross into Spain, Constantine III's general, Gerontius, rebels proclaiming Maximus as Western Emperor, coup against Constantine III's officials in Britain, Britain now permanently out of the Empire.
AD 411	Gerontius besieges Constantine III in Arles; Honorius' general, Constantius, eliminates both Gerontius and Constantine III.
AD 413	The last of the Gallic Emperors, Jovinus, is executed and the Gallic officials and military officers purged.

Independent Britain

AD 410	London abandoned, elite specialisation such as pottery manufacturing centres cease.
AD 420	Coins stop circulating.
AD 425	First Saxon migrants.
AD 441	*Chronica Gallica* of 452 claims Britain ruled by Saxons: this probably refers to Saxon migrations onto the south and east coasts and possibly up the rivers.
AD 536	Widespread agricultural failure caused by reduction in solar radiation probably as a result of a volcanic eruption.
AD 541–549	Plague of Justinian.
AD 600	Named heroic kings and their activities are history rather than myth, for example Penda (Saxon name) of Mercia, Cenwalh (British name?) of Wessex, Edwin (Saxon name) of Northumbria and Cadwallon (British name) of Gwynedd; Saxon kingdoms have elites and social hierarchies.
AD 670(?)	Tribal Hidage of the thirty-five tribes of Mercia and surrounds is compiled.
AD 700+	Mid Saxon Shift of settlements into valleys with rich soil.
AD 750+	Change from 'topographic' to 'land ownership' Saxon place names.
AD 800	Admixture between Brythonic and Saxon populations detectable in modern British genomes.
AD 800+	Brythonic largely eliminated from lowland Britain.

Bibliography

Abbott, D.H., Biscaye, P., Cole-Dai, J., Breger, D., 2008, 'Magnetite and Silicate Spherules from the GISP2 Core at the 536 A.D. Horizon.' AGU Fall Meeting Abstracts, 41: 41B–1454.

Adams, G., 2005. *Romano-Celtic Elites and their Religion*, Caeros Pty Ltd.

Alcock J.P., 2011. *A Brief History of Roman Britain Conquest and Civilization*, Constable & Robinson.

Anderson, H., 2013. 'The return to hill forts in the Dark Ages: what can this tell us about post-Roman Britain.' MA Thesis, University of Wales.

Arnold, C.J. & Wardle, P., 1981. 'Early Medieval Settlement Patterns in England', *Medieval Archaeology* 25, 145–9.

Bang, P.F., 2008. *The Roman Bazaar: A Comparative Study of Trade and Markets in a Tributary Empire*. Cambridge University Press.

Barbujani, G. & Sokal, R.R., 1990. 'Zones of sharp genetic change in Europe are also linguistic boundaries.' *Proceedings of the National Academy of Sciences of the USA*. 87(5): 1816–9.

Birley, A.R., 2005. *The Roman Government of Britain*, Oxford University Press

Birley, A.R., 2006. 'Britain during the Third Century Crisis.' in: Hekster, O., de Kleijn, G. & Slootjes, D. (eds.) *Crises and the Roman Empire*, Brill.

Birley, A., 2014. 'Brigomaglos and Riacus: A Brave New World? The Balance of Power at Post-Roman Vindolanda.' in: Haarer, F.K., (ed), *AD 410: The History and Archaeology of Late and Post-Roman Britain*. Malet Street: Society for the Promotion of Roman Studies.

Blair, J., 2014. 'In search of the origins of the English village.' *Current Archaeology*, 291:

Brace, S., Diekmann, Y. & Barnes, I., 2019. 'Ancient genomes indicate population replacement in Early Neolithic Britain.' *Nature Ecology & Evolution* 3: 765–71.

Breeze, D.J., 2003. 'Warfare in Britain and the Building of Hadrian's Wall.' *Archaeologia Aeliana* Series 5., 32: 13–16.

Breeze, D.J., 2006. *The Antonine Wall*. Birlinn Ltd.

Buckley, B.M., Anchukaitis, K.J., Penny, D., Fletcher, R., Cook, E.R., Sano, M., Nam, L.C., Wichienkeeo, A., Minh, T.T., & Hong, T.M., 2010. 'Climate as a contributing factor in the demise of Angkor, Cambodia.' *PNAS* April 13, 2010, 107 (15) 6748–52

Budd, P., Millard, A., Chenery, C., Lucy, S., & Roberts, C., 2004. 'Investigating population movement by stable isotope analysis: a report from Britain.' *Antiquity*, 78 (299). 127–41.

Brughmans, T., & Poblome, J., 2016. 'Roman bazaar or market economy? Explaining tableware distributions through computational modelling.' *Antiquity*, 90 (350): 393–408.

Burrows, M.H., 2017. 'Lower-class Violence in the Late Antique West.' Ph.D. Thesis, University of Leeds.

Butcher, K., 2015. 'Debasement and the decline of Rome.' in: Bland, R. & Calomino, D., (eds.) *Studies in ancient coinage in honor of Andrew Burnett*. Spink.

Charles-Edwards, T.M., 2012. *Wales and the Britons, 350–1064*, OUP.

Christiansen, B., Ljungqvist, F.C., 2012. 'The extra-tropical Northern Hemisphere temperature in the last two millennia: reconstructions of low-frequency variability.' *Climate Past*, 8: 765–86.

Cleere, H., 1977. 'The Classis Britannica.' in: Johnson, D.E., (ed.) *The Saxon Shore*. CBA Research Report No. 18: 16–19.

Coello, T.A., 1994. 'Unit Sizes in the Late Roman Army.' Open University PhD Thesis.

Couper, J.G., 2016. 'Gallic Insurgencies? Annihilating the Bagaudae.' in: Howe, T, Brice, L.L., (eds.) *Brill's companion to insurgency and terrorism in the ancient Mediterranean*. Brill.

Crummy, P., 1997. *City of Victory: Story of Colchester – Britain's First Roman Town*. Colchester Archaeological Trust.

Dando-Collins, S., 2010. *Legions of Rome: the definitive history of every Roman legion*. Quercus.

Dickinson, T.M., 1977. 'The Anglo-Saxon burial sites of the upper Thames region, and their bearing on the history of Wessex, circa AD 400–70', PhD Thesis, Oxford University.

Drake, B.L., 2017. 'Changes in North Atlantic Oscillation drove Population Migrations and the Collapse of the Western Roman Empire.' *Nature – Scientific Reports* 7, Article 1227.

Drews, R., 1993. *The End of the bronze age*. Princeton University Press.

Ebenesersdóttir, S.S., *et al* 2018. 'Ancient genomes from Iceland reveal the making of a human population.' *Science* 360: 1028–32

Elliott, S., 2016. *Sea Eagles of Empire*, The History Press.

Elliott, S., 2017a. 'Change and continuity in the exploitation of natural resources (such as stone, iron, clay and wood) in the principal areas of industrial activity in Kent (namely the Weald, Folkestone region and upper Medway Valley) during the Roman occupation.' PhD thesis, University of Kent.

Elliott, S., 2017b. *Empire State, how the Roman military built an empire*. Oxbow Books.

Elliott, S., 2018. *Septimius Severus in Scotland*. Greenhill Books.

Elliot, S., 2020. *Romans at War, The Roman Military in the Republic and Empire.* Casemate.

Elliott, S., 2021. *Roman Britain's Lost Legion: Whatever happened to Legio IX Hispana.* Pen & Sword.

Elliott, S., (in press). *Carausius.* Pen & Sword.

Elton, H., 1996. *Warfare in Roman Europe AD 350–425.* Oxford University Press.

Esmonde Cleary, A.S., 2003. 'Civil Defences in the West under the High Empire.' in: *The Archaeology of Roman Towns: studies in honour of John Watcher* (ed P. Wilson), Oxbow Books: 72–85.

Evans, N.P., Bauska, T.K., Gázquez-Sánchez, F., Brenner, M., Curtis, J.H., David A., Hodell, D.A., 2018. 'Quantification of drought during the collapse of the classic Maya civilization.' *Science* 361: 498–501.

Faulkner, N., 1996. 'Verulamium: Interpreting Decline.' *Archaeological Journal* 153: 79–103.

Finley, M.I., 1973. *The Ancient Economy.* University of California Press.

Fleming, R., 2010. *Britain after Rome.* Ian Allen.

Fonseca, V.G., Carvalho, G.R., Sung, W., Johnson, H.F., Power, D.M., Neill, S.P., Packer, M., Blaxter, M.L., Lambshead, P.J.D., Thomas, W.K., & Creer, S., 2010. 'Second-generation environmental sequencing unmasks marine metazoan biodiversity.' *Nature Communications* 1: 98pp.

Frend, W.H.C., 1992. 'Pagans, Christians and the 'barbarian conspiracy' of AD 367 in Roman Britain.' *Britannia* 23: 121–31.

Frere, S.S., 1984. 'The cities of Britain in the crisis of the third century.' *Revue Archéologique de Picardie* 3–4: 239–44.

Frere, S.S., 1991. *Britannia, a history of Roman Britain.* Pimlico.

Gelling, M. & Cole, A., 2000. *The Landscape of Place-Names.* Stamford.

Gibbard, P., 2007. 'Palaeogeography: Europe cut adrift', *Nature,* 448: 259–60.

Going, C. & Boast, R., 1994. 'Living traditions: continuity and change, past and present.' *Cambridge Journal of Anthropology* 17 (2): 103–18.

Goldsworthy, A., 2003. *Complete Roman Army.* Blackwells.

Graafstal, E., 2018. 'What Happened in the Summer of A.D.122? Hadrian on the British Frontier – Archaeology, Epigraphy and Historical Agency.' *Britannia* 49: 79–111.

Gupta, S., Collier, J.S., Palmer-Felgate, A. & Potter, G., 2007. 'Catastrophic flooding origin of shelf valley systems in the English Channel', *Nature,* 342–5.

Haak, W., Lazaridis, I., & Reich, D., 2015. 'Massive migration from the steppe was a source for Indo-European languages in Europe.' *Nature, Nature Research,* 522: 207–11.

Halsall, G.R.W., 2013a. *Worlds of Arthur: Facts and Fictions of the Dark Ages,* Oxford University Press.

Halsall, G.R.W., 2013b. 'Northern Britain and the Fall of the Roman Empire.' *The Medieval Journal.*

Hamerow, H.F., 1991. 'Settlement mobility and the 'Middle Saxon Shift: rural settlements and settlement patterns in Anglo-Saxon England.' *Anglo-Saxon England* 20: 1–17.

Hanley, R., 2000. *Villages in Roman Britain*. Shire Archaeology.

Hanson, W.S., 2020. 'The Design of the Antonine wall.' *Britannia* 51: 203–23.

Harper, K., 2017. *The Fate of Rome*. Princeton Press.

Harper, K. & McCormick, M., 2018. 'Reconstructing the Roman Climate.' in Schiedel, W., (ed) *The science of Roman History*. Princeton University Press. pp 11–52.

Heather, P., 2005. *The Fall of The Roman Empire*, Macmillan.

Helgason, A., Sigureth ardóttir, S., Nicholson, J., Sykes, B., Hill, E.W., Bradley, D.G., Bosnes, V., Gulcher, J.R., Ward, R., & Stefánsson, K., 2000. 'Estimating Scandinavian and Gaelic ancestry in the male settlers of Iceland.' *Am J Hum Genet.* 67(3): 697–717.

Hern, A.R.T., 2013. 'Soldiers and Society in Late Roman Belgica.' M.Phil Thesis, Manchester University.

Hind, J.G.F., 1977. 'The 'Genounian' Part of Britain.' *Britannia*, 8: 229–34.

Hingley, R., 2018. *Londinium: a biography: Roman London from its origins to the Fifth Century*, Illustrator C. Unwin, Bloomsbury Academic.

Hoffman, B., 2017. 'Hadrian's *Expeditio Britannica* – a new look at its historical and archaeological context.' Hadrianus MCM International Conference.

Hoggett, R., 2001. 'The origin and early development of Sedgeford, Norfolk.' MA thesis, University of Bristol.

Horn, S., 2012, 'Target enrichment via DNA hybridization capture.' *Methods in Molecular Biology*. 840: 177–88.

Horwath, R., 2006. 'The origin of strategy.' Strategic Thinking Institute.

Hough, C., 2004. 'The (non?) – survival of Romano-British toponymy.' *Neuphilologische Mitteilungen*, 105: 25–32

Jackson, R. & Potter T.W., 1996. *Excavations at Stonea, Cambridgeshire, 1980–85*. British Museum Press.

Jones, M., 1987. 'The failure of Romanization in Celtic Britain.' *Proceedings of the Harvard Celtic Colloquium*, 7: 126–45.

Keller, M., *et al*, 2019. 'Ancient Yersinia pestis genomes from across Western Europe reveal early diversification during the First Pandemic (541–750).' *Proceedings of the National Academy of Sciences*, 116 (25), 12363–7.

Koch, J.T., 2006. *Celtic culture: a historical encyclopaedia*. ABC-CLIO.

Lambshead, P.J.D., 1986. 'Sub-catastrophic sewage and industrial-waste contamination as revealed by marine nematode faunal analysis.' *Marine Ecology* – Progress Series 29, 247–60.

Langergraber, K., *et al*, 2012. 'Generation times in wild chimpanzees and gorillas suggest earlier divergence times in great ape and human evolution.' *PNAS* 109: 15716–21.

Lane, A., 2014. 'Wroxeter and the end of Roman Britain.' *Antiquity* 88: 501–15

Laycock, S., 2012. *Britannia: The Failed State: Tribal Conflicts and the End of Roman Britain*. The History Press.

Leslie *et al*, 2015. 'The fine scale genetic structure of the British population.' *Nature*, 519: 309–14.

Luttwak, E., 1976. *The Grand Strategy of the Roman Empire from the First Century A.D. to the Third*. John Hopkins University Press.

Markmann, M. & Tautz, D, Marsden, P., 1994. 'Ships of the Port of London, first to eleventh centuries AD.' *English Heritage Archaeological Report* 3.

Marsden, P. 1972. 'Blackfriars Wreck III: A Preliminary Note.' *International Journal of Nautical Archaeology* 1: 130–32.

Mason, D.J.P., 2003. *Roman Britain and the Roman Navy*. History Press.

Mattingly, D., 2006. *An Imperial Possession, Britain in the Roman Empire*. London, Penguin.

Millett, M., 1990. *The Romanisation of Britain*. Cambridge University Press.

Moorehead S., & Walton, P., 2014. 'Coinage at the End of Roman Britain.' in: Haarer, F.K., (ed), *AD 410: The History and Archaeology of Late and Post-Roman Britain*. Malet Street: Society for the Promotion of Roman Studies.

Mordechai, L., Eisenberg, M., Newfield, T.P., Izdebski, A., Kay, J.E., Poinar, H., 2019. 'The Justinianic Plague: An inconsequential pandemic?' *Proceedings of the National Academy of Sciences* 116 (51): 25546–54.

Moss, G., 2017. 'Brill's Companion to Insurgency and Terrorism in the Ancient Mediterranean. Brill's Companions in Classical Studies: Warfare in the Ancient Mediterranean World.' *Bryan Mawr Classical Review*.

O'Kelly, M.J., 1989. *Early Ireland, an Introduction to Irish Prehistory*. Cambridge University Press.

Oltean, I., 2007. *Dacia: Landscape, Colonization and Romanization*. Routledge.

Pearson, A., 2002. *Coastal Defences of Southern Britain*. Tempus Publishing Ltd.

Papworth, M., 2021. 'The case for Chedworth villa. Exploring evidence of 5th Century occupation.' *Current Archaeology* 373: 18–25.

Perring, D., 2017. 'London's Hadrianic War.' *Britannia*, 48: 37–76.

Perring, D., 2011. 'Population Decline and Ritual Landscapes in Antonine London.' *Journal of Roman Archaeology*, 24: 249–66.

Perring, D., 2015. 'Recent Advances in the Understanding of Roman London.' in: *The Towns of Roman Britain: The Contribution of Commercial Archaeology Since 1990*, Britannia Monograph No. 27.

Potter, T.W., and Whitehouse, D.B., 1982. 'A Roman Building in the Cambridgeshire Fens, and Some Parallels near Rome.' *World Archaeology* 14: 218–23.

Pryor, F., 2004. *Britain AD, A quest for Arthur, England and the Anglo-Saxons*. Harper Perennial.

Rascovan, N., Sjögren, K-G., Kristiansen, K., Nielsen, R., Willerslev, E., Desnues, C., Rasmussen, S., 2019. 'Emergence and Spread of Basal Lineages of Yersinia pestis during the Neolithic Decline.' *Cell* 176 (2): 295–305.

Rathbone., D., 1996. 'Monetisation not Price Inflation, in Third Century Egypt.' in: King, C.E. & Wigg, D.G. (eds.) *Coin Finds and Coin Use in the Roman World*. Gebr. Mann Verlag.

Reece, R., 'Roman Currency, New Thoughts and Problems.' *World Archaeology* 6: 299–306.

Reece, R., 1997. 'The Future of Roman Military Archaeology.' The Tenth Annual Caerleon Lecture, Cardiff.

Reno, W., 2014. 'Insurgent Movements in Africa.' in Rich, P.B. & Duyvesteyn, I., (eds.), *Routledge Handbook of Insurgency and Counterinsurgency*. Routledge.

Richmond, I.A., 'Roman and Native in the Fourth Century.' in: Richmond, I.A., (ed.) *Roman and Native in North Britain*. Nelson.

Salway, P., 1993. *The Oxford Illustrated History of Roman Britain*. Butler & Tanner.

Sánchez-Quinto, F. *et al*, 2012. 'Genomic Affinities of Two 7,000-Year-Old Iberian Hunter-Gatherers.' *Current Biology* 22 (16): 1494–9.

Scheidel, W., 2014. 'The shape of the Roman World: modelling Roman connectivity.' *Journal of Roman Archaeology* 27: 7–32.

Shaw, B.D., 2004. 'Bandits in the Roman Empire.' in: Osborne, R., (ed.) *Studies in Ancient Greek and Roman Society*. Cambridge University Press.

Smith, A., 1776. *The Wealth of Nations*, W. Strahan and T. Cadell.

Southern, P., & Dixon, K.R., 1996. *The Late Roman Army*. BT Batsford Ltd.

Spyrou, Maria A., Tukhbatova, R.I., Chuan-Chao, W., Valtueña, A.A., Lankapalli, A.K., Kondrashin, V.V.; Tsybin, V.A., Khokhlov, A.K.D., Herbig, A., Bos, Kirsten I., Krause, J., 2018. 'Analysis of 3800-year-old Yersinia pestis genomes suggests Bronze Age origin for bubonic plague.' *Nature Communications*. 9 (#1): 2234

Stathakopoulos, D., 2018. 'Plague, Justinianic (Early Medieval Pandemic).' *The Oxford Dictionary of Late Antiquity*, Oxford University Press.

Thompson, E.A., 1982. *Romans and Barbarians: The Decline of the Western Empire*. University of Wisconsin Press.

Tomlin, R.S.O., 1979. 'Graffiti on Roman bricks and tiles found in Britain.' in: McWhirr, A. (ed) *Roman Brick and Tile*, British Archaeological Reports, International Series, 68.

Trithemié, J., 1873. *Les Bagaudes et les origines de la Nation Française*.

Van Ossel, P., 1995. 'Insécurité et militarization en Gaule du Nord au Bas-Empire. L'exemple des campagnes', *Revue du Nord-Archeologie*, 77: 27–36.

Visbeck, M.H., Hurrell, J. W., Polvani, L., Cullen, H.M., 2001. 'The North Atlantic Oscillation: Past, present and future.' *PNAS* 98: 12876–77.

Wallace-Hadrill, A., 2008. *Rome's Cultural Revolution*, Cambridge.

Walton, P., & Moorehead, S., 2016. 'Coinage and Collapse. The contribution of numismatic data to understanding the end of Roman Britain', *Internet Archaeology* 41.

Ward-Perkins, B., 2005. *The fall of Rome and the end of civilisation*. Oxford University Press.

Watanabe, T.K., Watanabe, T., Yamazaki, A., Pfeiffer, M., 2019. 'Oman corals suggest that a stronger winter shamal season caused the Akkadian Empire (Mesopotamia) collapse.' *Geology*, 47 (12): 1141–5.

West H., Quinn, N., Horswell, M., 2019. 'Regional rainfall response to the North Atlantic Oscillation (NAO) across Great Britain.' *Hydrology Research*, 50 (6): 1549–63.

White, R.H., 2007. *Britannia Prima: Britain's last Roman province*. Tempus.

Wilkes, J.J., 1963. 'A Note on the Mutiny of the Pannonian Legions in A.D. 14.' *The Classical Quarterly*, 13 (2): 268–71.

Woodcock, R., 2016. 'Language Contact and Identity in Roman Britain', MA Thesis, University of Western Ontario.

Woods, D., 2012. 'On the alleged letters of Honorius to the British cities in 410.' *Latomus* 71: 818–26.

Ziskowski, A., 2007. 'Debating the Origins of Colonial Women in Sicily and South Italy.' *ElAnt* 11, 1

Acknowledgements

I would like to thank Simon Elliot for his inspirational help and probing discussion at all stages of this project. I must also thank Oliver Gilkes for a peer-group review of the final draft. Needless to say, these scholars should not be blamed for such errors and inadequacies as remain as these must be laid at my door.